D1521424

UNSETTLING WORSHIP

WORSHIP AND WITNESS

The Worship and Witness series seeks to foster a rich, interdisciplinary conversation on the theology and practice of public worship, a conversation that will be integrative and expansive. Integrative, in that scholars and practitioners from a wide range of disciplines and ecclesial contexts will contribute studies that engage church and academy. Expansive, in that the series will engage voices from the global church and foreground crucial areas of inquiry for the vitality of public worship in the twenty-first century.

The Worship and Witness series demonstrates and cultivates the interaction of topics in worship studies with a range of crucial questions, topics, and insights drawn from other fields. These include the traditional disciplines of theology, history, and pastoral ministry—as well as cultural studies, political theology, spirituality, and music and the arts. The series focus will thus bridge church worship practices and the vital witness these practices nourish.

We are pleased that you have chosen to join us in this conversation, and we look forward to sharing this learning journey with you.

Series Editors:
John D. Witvliet
Noel Snyder
Maria Cornou

UNSETTLING WORSHIP

Reforming Liturgy for Right Relations with Indigenous Communities

Sarah Travis

CASCADE *Books* · Eugene, Oregon

UNSETTLING WORSHIP
Reforming Liturgy for Right Relations with Indigenous Communities

Worship and Witness

Cascade Books
An Imprint of Wipf and Stock Publishers
199 W. 8th Ave., Suite 3
Eugene, OR 97401

www.wipfandstock.com

PAPERBACK ISBN: 978-1-6667-4661-7
HARDCOVER ISBN: 978-1-6667-4662-4
EBOOK ISBN: 978-1-6667-4663-1

Cataloguing-in-Publication data:

Names: Travis, Sarah, author.

Title: Unsettling Worship: reforming liturgy for right relations with indigenous communities / by Sarah Travis.

Description: Eugene, OR: Cascade Books, 2023 | Series: Worship and Witness | Includes bibliographical references.

Identifiers: ISBN 978-1-6667-4661-7 (paperback) | ISBN 978-1-6667-4662-4 (hardcover) | ISBN 978-1-6667-4663-1 (ebook)

Subjects: LCSH: Worship. | Indigenous people—North American—Religion.

Classification: E98.R3 T73 2023 (paperback) | E98.R3 (ebook)

VERSION NUMBER 081523

All Scripture quotations, unless otherwise noted, are from The New Revised Standard Version Bible (NRSV), Copyright 1989, Division of Christian Education of the National Council of the Churches of Christ in the United States of America.

"Shannen and the Attiwapiskat School" used with permission of the Presbyterian Church in Canada.

For the children.

CONTENTS

ACKNOWLEDGMENTS

THE WORK OF CONCILIATION/RECONCILIATION is a collective task, and the writing of this book is no exception. It all began with a teacher-scholar grant from the Calvin Institute for Christian Worship, which supported this project and allowed me to gather a group of consultants to work alongside me. I am profoundly grateful to Margaret Mullin, Lori Ransom, Brian Fraser, and Germaine Lovelace for accompanying me with grace and wisdom. Their insights are woven through these pages, although not always acknowledged. Know that you have inspired and formed me by your warmth and great love for one another even as we discussed very challenging realities. Thank you to Knox College, University of Toronto, for administering the grant. Thank you to Michael Thompson at Wipf and Stock for being a willing sounding-board and encouraging me to continue to tackle challenging topics. Thank you to Lianne Biggar for her always fabulous copyediting.

The support and encouragement of my husband, Paul Miller, are unwavering. Paul, I am eternally grateful for your partnership on this journey. Olive and Ella, thank you for sharing your mum with this project. Ben Travis-Miller, you always inspire me toward a greater sense of justice. Thank you for engaging with parts of this manuscript and always challenging my assumptions and perceptions. I am so proud of you.

These pages contain a great deal of shame and sorrow but also hope for a better world. For denominations and individual citizens, there is work to be done. My prayer is that this project will interrupt settler patterns and engagements with Indigenous peoples, so that we may create relationships that are mutually respectful and generous. While I have approached this project with a spirit of humility, I ask forgiveness for those times when my own fragility or lack of understanding blot these pages. As the earth groans in labor pains, we hear the divine promise that there is life beyond what we have prepared for and imagined. May it be so, for the children's sake.

INTRODUCTION

IN THE NINETEENTH AND twentieth centuries, Indigenous children were forcibly removed from their homes and communities and sent to institutions that were tasked with "removing the Indian from the child," words attributed to Canada's first prime minister, John A. Macdonald. In the late 1800s, Macdonald is quoted as saying:

> When the school is on the reserve, the child lives with its parents, who are savages [*sic*], and though he may learn to read and write, his habits and training mode of thought are Indian. He is simply a savage [*sic*] who can read and write. . . . Indian children should be withdrawn as much as possible from the parental influence, and the only way to do that would be to put them in central training industrial schools where they will acquire the habits and modes of thought of white men.[1]

Residential "schools" were established by the Canadian government and Christian churches. The goal of residential schools was assimilation, if not the outright destruction of Indigenous populations and cultures. It is estimated that many thousands of children died in residential schools, although many graves remain undisclosed. While many of these deaths were caused by illness and disease, there is a sinister probability that many died because of abuse and intentional neglect.

In the spring of 2021, the remains of 215 children were located at the former site of a residential school in Kamloops, British Columbia. While Indigenous communities have always known that many of their children never came home, the discovery of the bodies brought the truth to light for those Canadians who had little or no knowledge of residential schools. When the news broke about the uncovering of the children's bodies, the nation was caught off guard and struggled to respond appropriately. Settler Canadians felt grief for Indigenous communities, which were devastated by

---

1. Macdonald, *Official Report of the Debates*, 1107–8.

the confirmation of the children's deaths. Settler Canadians also felt other things—shame and guilt for the role of settlers in the process, anger toward churches and governments, indifference, especially for those who knew nothing of this system that resulted in the horrors that are now before us. Some have denied the existence of the bodies or become angry at the very idea that they bear any responsibility toward Indigenous communities. A wave of orange swept the country as people purchased orange shirts or left teddy bears on their doorsteps in order to honor the children.[2] For worship leaders, it was a moment of confusion and anxiety. What could we possibly say or do in the face of such horror? Despite the difficulties, this horror had to be addressed in the context of Christian worship. Worship leaders scrambled to find the words and actions to respond to such deep trauma. "Thoughts and prayers" are not enough.

Worship leaders and preachers have the ongoing challenge of address-ing the realities of human life. War, natural disasters, disease, violence—we must speak into the void and into the chaos, into this "grim fabric of life."[3] We are invited to interpret the world through the lens of the gospel. The gospel consistently calls us toward truth-telling and reconciliation. Worship is a space in which to consider both the very worst that human beings are capable of and the very best. It is a space in which we are formed by the forgiveness of God in order to be made free to imagine better, stronger rela-tionships. In Canada and other nations, the relationship of settler churches to Indigenous peoples is a significant area of concern. Seeking right rela-tions is an urgent task because the damage has been immense. The lives of Indigenous folk literally depend on the manner in which settlers respond and repair the damage that has been done by generations of colonialism.

Canada has undergone a process of Truth and Reconciliation simi-lar to that which occurred in South Africa after the end of apartheid. As a result, the Truth and Reconciliation Commission of Canada (TRC) issued ninety-four Calls to Action, which offer a means for Canadians, including the parties of the Settlement Agreement, to respond to the TRC's findings.[4] The Settlement Agreement represents the consensus reached between legal counsel for former residential school students, Churches, the Assembly

2. Orange Shirt Day originates from the story of Phyllis Webstad from the Stswecem'c Xgat'tem First Nation. In 1973, on her first day at residential school, a new orange shirt given to her by her grandmother was taken away from her, and she was forced to wear the clothing provided. Forty years later, on September 30, 2013, Phyllis spoke publicly for the first time about her experience, and thus began the Orange Shirt Day movement. See https://www.orangeshirtday.org/ for more information.

3. Presbyterian Church in Canada, *Living Faith*, introduction.

4. Truth and Reconciliation Commission, "Calls to Action."

of First Nations, other Indigenous organizations, and the government of Canada.[5] Call to Action number fifty-nine reads, "We call upon church parties to the Settlement Agreement to develop ongoing education strategies to ensure that their respective congregations learn about their church's role in colonization, the history and legacy of residential schools, and why apologies to former residential school students, their families, and communities were necessary."[6]

Canadian churches have accepted a responsibility to teach about colonization and its implications, not only because they are parties to the Settlement Agreement but also because reconciliation is an imperative for Christians. In worship, our identities as children of God are formed and expressed. Worship takes us on a journey as we gather, confess, hear the word and preach it, consider it, celebrate the sacraments, and are sent out into the world to live out what we have experienced within the context of worship. It is a space to consider our histories and varied identities as well as our relationships with God and with others. According to the final report of the TRC, "For churches, demonstrating long-term commitment requires atoning for actions within the residential schools, respecting Indigenous spirituality, and supporting Indigenous peoples' struggles for justice and equity."[7]

This book explores the question, How does worship prepare us to engage in the work of conciliation/reconciliation with Indigenous peoples? Using a framework of fourfold worship, I consider the ways that our worship gives space to examine and improve our relationships—not only with Indigenous peoples but also with all those we consider "other." I begin with the assumption that worship is a formative practice for Christians. It shapes us in particular ways to be sent into the world as ambassadors of reconciliation.[8] Christians often come to worship to "feel better" or more comfortable. The great challenge of decolonizing worship is that it will make us uncomfortable. Worship is designed to unsettle us—we should be disturbed by the word of God. Reconciliation is a word that should disturb us because it requires leaving behind comfortable spaces and entering into relationships that are fraught because of historical and contemporary colonialism and racism. None of this is easy. God's word and activity in worship are disruptive—they interrupt our systems and our plans.

5. Government of Canada, Indian Residential Schools Settlement Agreement.

6. Truth and Reconciliation Commission, "Calls to Action."

7. Truth and Reconciliation Commission, *Canada's Residential Schools*, 21.

8. 2 Cor 5:18, 20.

Defining Terms

Terminology is a somewhat thorny issue for this project. Terms such as *reconciliation* and *settler* are heavily loaded; they carry a great deal of meaning that may or may not correlate to the reality of lived experience. I want to be clear about how I am choosing the terminology that grounds this project. "Dialogue requires terminology we can use to name one another, so we can recognize how certain events impacted/impact us differently, as well as what we have in common as diverse peoples."[9] While these categories are messy and leaking, they will help us to lay a foundation for the kinds of conversations that will be convened in this book.

Reconciliation is the common term for referring to the process of seeking right relations among Indigenous and non-Indigenous peoples. The TRC has clearly chosen to use the term *reconciliation* to describe this process, defining it as "being about establishing and maintaining a mutually respectful relationship between Aboriginal and non-Aboriginal peoples . . . for that to happen, there has to be awareness of the past, acknowledgement of the harm that has been inflicted, atonement for the causes, and actions to change behaviour."[10] Reconciliation is not possible without an accounting of the wrongs committed and a genuine commitment to change both attitudes and behaviors. One of the challenges of the term *reconciliation* is that it presumes that there is an existing relationship that can be repaired. This is not the case in Canada—some would argue that there is not, and has never been, a positive relationship between settlers and Indigenous peoples. Mark Charles and Soong Chan Rah write:

> Because the more familiar term racial reconciliation implies a pre-existing harmony and unity, we propose the use of the term racial conciliation. Conciliation does not happen without truth telling. Conciliation without truth is trying to bring health without a comprehensive diagnosis. Truth telling requires the deeper examination of the existing narratives and the unearthing of the dysfunction surrounding those narratives.[11]

There is no question here that reconciliation, or conciliation, requires the hard work of truth-telling and listening. The TRC reports that Elders and Knowledge Keepers have stated that there is no specific word for reconciliation in Indigenous languages. Instead, there are "many words, stories and songs, as well as sacred objects such as wampum belts, peace pipes, eagle

9. âpihtawikosisân, "Settling on a Name."

10. Truth and Reconciliation Commission, *Canada's Residential Schools*, 6–7.

11. Charles and Rah, *Unsettling Truths*, loc. 154.

down, cedar boughs, drums and regalia, that are used to establish relationships, repair conflicts, restore harmony, and make peace."[12] These words, stories, songs, and sacred objects form part of the Indigenous response to the hope for right relations.

Willie Jennings writes of the challenge of the term *reconciliation*, explaining, "I have purposely stayed away from the theological language of reconciliation because of its terrible misuse in Western Christianity and its tormented deployment in so many theological systems and projects. The concept of reconciliation is not irretrievable, but. . . . In truth, it is not at all clear that most Christians are ready to imagine reconciliation."[13] Reconciliation has been used as a theological weapon: for example, when it is employed to force victims/survivors into relationship with their oppressors. It is often assumed that reconciliation can occur without the costly work of confession and repentance—both of which are prerequisites for genuine reconciliation. Those who call for unity and peace without justice and accountability are not really preaching reconciliation.

I am reluctant to let go of the language of reconciliation entirely, as it is used so broadly to describe the kind of work for which I am advocating here. It perfectly describes the relationship between God and creation. It less perfectly describes our human relationships, especially those among Indigenous and non-Indigenous peoples. Thus, I will use the term *reconciliation* (particularly when describing God's action) and *reconciliation/conciliation* (more commonly when describing human endeavor). I have also chosen the term *right relations* as a way of naming the hope of conciliation, that those who are distant from one another may find a way to relate to each other in a mutually respectful process. Right relations is not merely about generosity on the part of settlers; it is a deep recognition that Indigenous peoples come as equals and bring enormous gifts to the table. The church continues to act as a colonizer toward Indigenous peoples, and those patterns must change if conciliation/reconciliation is to occur. It is also essential to name another partner in this process—the earth itself. The TRC repeatedly heard that reconciliation is not possible unless we are first reconciled to creation, which continues to be broken by human communal sin.[14]

Another difficult task is describing the groups of people we are concerned with—those who were the first to occupy the lands that we now call North America, and those who came later, associated with the conquering of the land. While the TRC uses the terms *aboriginal* and *non-aboriginal*, as

12. Truth and Reconciliation Commission, *Canada's Residential Schools*, 17.

13. Jennings, *Christian Imagination*, loc. 253–59.

14. Truth and Reconciliation Commission, *Canada's Residential Schools*, 18.

well as *Indigenous*, I gravitate toward the term *Indigenous*. No language can adequately capture the diversity and beauty of Indigenous communities, and I do not wish to collapse the identity of nations into a single word. When I use the term Indigenous, I am referring specifically to those groups that identity themselves as First Nations, Métis, or Inuit. In the United States, *Native American* may be a more popular term. The United Nations does not define *Indigenous* per se, instead relying on the following descriptors:

- Self-identification as Indigenous peoples at the individual level and accepted by the community as their member
- Historical continuity with precolonial and/or pre-settler societies
- Strong link to territories and surrounding natural resources
- Distinct social, economic, or political systems
- Distinct language, culture, and beliefs
- Form non-dominant groups of society
- Resolve to maintain and reproduce their ancestral environments and systems as distinctive peoples and communities[15]

Since this is a book primarily for those who identify more with the colonizer than the colonized, the language we use to describe ourselves is very important. There is considerable debate about the terms *non-Indigenous*, *settler*, and *newcomer*. âpihtawikosisân argues that there is no generally accepted term to describe "the non-Indigenous peoples living in Canada who form the European-descended sociopolitical majority."[16] They go on: "Naming these peoples is just as important as naming Indigenous peoples if we are going to talk about how the past informs the present."[17] The available terms (*white*, *European*, *non-Indigenous*, *settler*) each have benefits and disadvantages. It is perhaps most useful to think of these terms according to the ways they describe relationality. *White*, while being an important descriptor and a category that requires significant reflection, excludes those who are not white. The same problem exists with the term *European*: It doesn't include those who are immigrants from other places in the world. Neither term adequately describes the relation between Indigenous peoples and others, such as recent immigrants. In addition, the terms *white* or *European* may be experienced as divisive or pejorative.[18] If we use the term non-Indigenous,

---

15. United Nations Permanent Forum, "Who Are Indigenous Peoples?"
16. âpihtawikosisân, "Settling on a Name."
17. âpihtawikosisân, "Settling on a Name."
18. âpihtawikosisân, "Settling on a Name."

we are simply defining somebody by what they are not. The term *newcomer* may be confusing—although it is intended to refer to those who came later to the land, it may be unclear whether it is referring to long-settled families or recent immigrants. The term *settler* may be most helpful here, as it is not a racial category, and it carries the emotional weight of relationship.[19]

Barker and Lowman argue that we need a name that "can help us see ourselves for who we are, not just who we claim to be. For that we need a term that shifts the frame of reference away from our nation, our claimed territory, and onto our relationships with systems of power, land, and the peoples on whose territory our country exists."[20] For them, *settler* mirrors the construction of the term *Indigenous* and refers to "a broad collective of peoples with commonalities through particular connections to land and place."[21] For settlers, these connections were often forged through violence and the displacement of Indigenous populations.[22] Barker and Lowman point to the many ways in which Canada remains colonial in its attitudes and actions toward Indigenous peoples. To embrace the term *settler* is to turn the Canadian gaze toward the reality that the problems with Indigenous relationships originated with the settlers, not with Indigenous peoples.[23] Settlers are apt to treat Indigenous peoples' resistance, and the protection of their lands, with hostility. However, the cause of the conflict is "the society that takes domination of Indigenous peoples for granted."[24] The term *settler* foregrounds issues of accountability, responsibility, and agency—it implies a deep moral responsibility that, as colonizers, we seek to heal our relationships with the land which we call home.[25] Settler identity is rooted in the practices of settler colonialism, which will be defined in chapter 1.

It is not possible to transcend these structures on our own. We cannot simply step outside of our settler identity, but we can become aware of the ways that we, individually and communally, benefit from and sustain systems of power.[26] *Settler* is not a pejorative word but simply a means of stating our identities as ones who have come to land in a particular way. Lowman and Barker perceive *settler* to be an interrogative word: When we are asked to identify as settler people, we are answering the questions, "How do you

---

19. âpihtawikosisân, "Settling on a Name."

20. Lowman and Barker, *Settler*, 1.

21. Lowman and Barker, *Settler*, 2.

22. Lowman and Barker, *Settler*, 2.

23. Lowman and Barker, *Settler*, 6.

24. Lowman and Barker, *Settler*, 9.

25. Lowman and Barker, *Settler*, 15.

26. Lowman and Barker, *Settler*, 16.

come to be here? How do you claim belonging here? And, most importantly, can we belong in a way that doesn't reproduce colonial dispossession and harm?"[27] In order to create respectful relationships, settlers should become familiar with Indigenous ways of knowing and their worldviews. None of this is a comfortable process. Settlers find themselves responsible for actions that were taken by someone else, sometimes many years ago. Anger, shame, and guilt are appropriate responses to colonization, and these emotions will almost certainly be stirred by the necessity of repairing what is broken. Settlers will learn from this discomfort, but they must carry it for themselves. As Jana-Rae Yerxa has explained, Indigenous people must not be expected to carry the burdens of settler discomfort.[28]

The final report of the Truth and Reconciliation Commission describes the process of assimilation which has occurred causing "Aboriginal peoples [sic] to cease to exist as distinct legal, social, cultural, religious and racial entities in Canada."[29] The residential schools system in particular was a project of cultural genocide, "the destruction of those structures and practices that allow the group to continue as a group."[30] This includes the destruction of political and social institutions, the seizure of land, the forbidding of native languages, the persecution of religious practices, and the manner in which families are disrupted from passing on cultural values to the next generation. While there is debate about the term cultural genocide, I believe that this is a fitting term to describe the destructive goals of colonialism, especially in the Canadian context. If we embrace the idea that Canada has participated in a project of cultural genocide, then our response becomes even more urgent, even as it is complicated and difficult.

Worship and Reconciliation/Conciliation

My framework builds upon the reformed worship tradition, which has a number of key principles or emphases. Reformed worship tends to be organized around four distinct movements: the gathering, the word, the response to the word, and the sending. As we gather, we are oriented toward the triune God, who calls us to worship in a particular time and place. This portion of the service also includes the essential act of confession and the assurance of pardon. The portion of worship that addresses the word includes the public reading of Scripture and the interpretation of the Scripture

27. Lowman and Barker, *Settler*, 19.

28. Yerxa, "Refuse to Live Quietly!"

29. Truth and Reconciliation Commission, *Canada's Residential Schools*, 1.

30. Truth and Reconciliation Commission, *Canada's Residential Schools*, 1.

in preaching. The response to the word contains the Sacraments of Holy Communion and baptism as well as the prayers of the people. Finally, in the Sending portion of the service, participants are sent out into the world to continue the worship that was begun collectively. When we are sent out, we recognize that we are formed and equipped to live out the gospel message in our own neighborhoods and communities as ambassadors of reconciliation.

The Calvin Institute for Christian Worship has identified ten key convictions about worship, reformed worship in particular. These convictions are useful in identifying the purpose and goal of reformed worship. Christian worshiping communities are diverse, but many in the reformed tradition rely on these convictions.

1. Awareness of the glory, beauty, and holiness of God.[31] Worship cultivates an awareness of God's identity and our own identity as children of God. The triune God is the focus of worship.

2. Full, conscious, active participation.[32] Through the Holy Spirit, all worshipers participate fully in the act of worship. Worship encompasses the whole people of God, regardless of age, culture, or status.

3. Deep engagement with Scripture.[33] We know of God's redemptive work in Jesus Christ because of scriptural revelation. Our worship should be grounded in the Scriptures of the Old and New Testaments. Worship should depict God in ways that are consistent with the stories of Scripture.

4. Celebrations of baptism and the Lord's Supper.[34] These are gifts of grace that form an essential aspect of worship. In baptism, we are cleansed of our sin and made free for a life of discipleship. At the communion table, we are fed and made ready to feed others.

5. A discerning approach to culture.[35] "Worship should strike a healthy balance among four approaches or dimensions to its cultural context: worship is transcultural (some elements of worship are beyond culture), contextual (worship reflects the culture in which it is offered), cross-cultural (worship breaks barriers of culture through worship),

---

31. Calvin Institute, "Ten Core Convictions."
32. Calvin Institute, "Ten Core Convictions."
33. Calvin Institute, "Ten Core Convictions."
34. Calvin Institute, "Ten Core Convictions."
35. Calvin Institute, "Ten Core Convictions."

and counter-cultural (worship resists the idolatries of its cultural context)."[36]

6. Disciplined creativity in the arts.[37] Art in all its forms, when used judiciously and faithfully, enhances the worship life of the congregation.

7. Collaboration with other ministries.[38] Worship is our primary task as God's people, but worship does not happen in a vacuum. It is mutually supported by pastoral care, education, and outreach.

8. Hospitality.[39] Worship breaks down barriers that exist between individuals and groups. We worship together regardless of our demographic or cultural differences.

9. Intentional integration with all of life.[40] Worship is connected to our daily lives. We are invited to reflect and act upon all aspects of our existence in light of the truth of the triune God. This will lead to conversations about issues such as restorative justice and creation care.

10. Collaboration in planning and evaluation.[41] Worship is a team effort, not just the work of a sole worship leader. By consulting with others, worship leaders are enabled to facilitate worship experiences that reflect the diversity of the gathered congregation.

While all of these convictions are important for shaping our understanding of reformed worship, some are especially relevant to the current project, which ponders worship as a space in which we are equipped and prepared for the work of conciling broken relationships. The triune God, as the center of our worship, is always pulling us toward reconciliation. God so loved the world that he sent Jesus Christ to pitch his tent among us, so that we might understand the depth of God's love and grace toward us. We find our own impetus for reconciliation in the very acts of God that reconciled us in Jesus Christ. I would argue that reconciliation is a goal for worship—we come to remember that we have been reconciled to God and that there is a need to be reconciled, or conciled, to others. Matthew 5, in the Sermon on the Mount, urges believers to repair broken relationships prior to bringing a gift to the altar. There is an assumption here that we will be conciled/reconciled to others before we worship. We know, however, that conciliation/reconciliation

36. Calvin Institute, "Ten Core Convictions."

37. Calvin Institute, "Ten Core Convictions."

38. Calvin Institute, "Ten Core Convictions."

39. Calvin Institute, "Ten Core Convictions."

40. Calvin Institute, "Ten Core Convictions."

41. Calvin Institute, "Ten Core Convictions."

is an ongoing project. In worship, we are formed as individuals and as a community to continue the work of conciling and reconciling relationships that have been destroyed by human sin. In worship, we are reminded of God's forgiveness in Jesus Christ, and through the agency of God we are made free to join in this conversation about the possibility of forgiveness within human relationships. This is the work to which Christians are called.

Hospitality is another key aspect of worship in terms of the work of reconciliation. When we gather for worship, we are invited to fully embrace all those with whom we share the worship experience, even when those people are significantly different from ourselves. As Cláudio Carvalhaes writes, "Liturgies, as privileged spaces for social entanglement, are marked by the condition of hosting the foreigner, the stranger, the parasite."[42] Worship is a space of hospitality, even for those who are different, unfamiliar, or unpleasant.

By enacting a faithful imagination, worshipers can also embrace those who are not in the worship space but who exist in parallel communities. We can be hospitable by acknowledging the human rights of others, including Indigenous communities. We can be hospitable by making space to encounter the stories of others within our worship—particularly through Scripture that opens us to the ways that people of faith have described their experiences with God; and through preaching that tells us about the experiences of others; and through prayer, which is a way of reaching beyond ourselves, and connecting with God as well as other human beings.

There is, of course, another aspect of the reformed tradition that is relevant here—the task of continually reforming the faith. By unsettling worship, we commit to an honest accounting of worship and imagine ways that it can be reformed in such a manner that it equips us for stronger relationships. A key question is how worship itself can be decolonized.

Decolonizing Worship

I am approaching worship and the topic of reconciliation through a decolonizing lens. Decolonizing theories and theologies examine the ways that texts and human relationships are impacted by historical and contemporary manifestations of colonialism and imperialism. Imperialism is an ideology of superiority, which claims that one nation or group has a divine right to rule another group or nation. Colonialism is a political practice that brings imperialism to life by exploiting the natural and human resources in a particular region. To examine worship from a decolonizing perspective is

42. Carvalhaes, *Liturgy in Postcolonial Perspectives*, 12.

to interrogate worship for remnants of imperial and colonial thought and practice. Claudio Carvalhaes argues that the "colonial presence" has shaped the discourse of many domains, including the practices of Christian liturgy.[43] Decolonized liturgical theologies "are ways in which praxis, theories, and theologies of religious groups are engaged in order to challenge those times when the imperial, colonizing power dynamics of domination use religious ideologies/reifications as instruments of an agenda of conquering and dismissal, undermining autonomies and destruction of people's lives, wisdom, and sovereignties."[44] This book intends to engage the practices of worship in order to strengthen, not undermine, people's lives, wisdom, and sovereignties. To that end, it is an attempt at decolonizing liturgy. "Liturgies are powerful actions that tell us what and how to think, what (not) to do, how and what (not) to relate to, what to avoid, and so on. Liturgical religious movements shape bodies, minds, spirits, politics, economies, and nation-states."[45] Carvalhaes reminds us that worship is always rooted in power by maintaining or opposing powers in their current formation and structure.[46] In other words, our liturgies shape, and are shaped by, the formations of power in our society. By working at the borders and boundaries of worship and culture, decolonizing liturgical theologies functions to challenge and dismantle structures of power. "The colonial discourse creates an identity that swallows difference and turns the multiplicity of the sacred into cultural uniformity and monotony."[47] Instead, we are called to find a way to honor difference and diversity and broaden our understanding of God's identity.

The term *third space* may be helpful here. Elsewhere, I have described worship as a third space in which we encounter God and others. In this space, there is room for dialogue and an acknowledgment of power and the ways that power disrupts equitable, positive relationships.

> If we imagine Third Space encounters to be located within a Trinitarian space, these encounters are not limited to the human persons or groups involved. Rather, they are indwelled by the Triune God, and thus opened to a Trinitarian discourse that deconstructs all other discourse. All binaries and us-versus-them are interrupted and decentered by the divine presence. At odds with the territorialism of colonialism and cultural imperialism, Third Spaces do not belong to one or the other, to

43. Carvalhaes, *Liturgy in Postcolonial Perspectives*, 1.
44. Carvalhaes, *Liturgy in Postcolonial Perspectives*, 2.
45. Carvalhaes, *Liturgy in Postcolonial Perspectives*, 3.
46. Carvalhaes, *Liturgy in Postcolonial Perspectives*, 4.
47. Carvalhaes, *Liturgy in Postcolonial Perspectives*, 9.

the Tricontinent or to the West, to the colonizer or colonized or observers. These spaces belong to God-in-Trinity.[48]

I invite the reader into a third space . . . a space where we examine our worship practices for abuses and misuses of power, the suppression of difference, and the potential for transformative change. While our cultures are still plagued by imperial ideologies, we are free to think beyond the present. The third space is brightened by hope and imagination. We hope that there is a way to be reconciled to God and to one another. We are equipped to imagine a new context for relationship, or perhaps even the rooting and grounding of brand-new relationships. Into this space, we invite a cacophony of voices—some familiar and some unfamiliar. These voices challenge us, deconstruct us, revise our well-loved liturgies, and draw us toward the distinctly uncomfortable work of partnering with God to remake the world. The goal is to reestablish an understanding of the interdependence of all of creation.

The Development of This Volume

This book has been written with the support of a teacher-scholar grant from the Calvin Institute for Christian Worship. My task is to write about Christian worship and the ways that worship can prepare us for the hard work of conciliation/reconciliation between settler Christians and Indigenous peoples who live in the territory politically defined as Canada. I am an ordained minister of The Presbyterian Church in Canada (PCC), which has a long history of involvement with residential schools. I teach preaching and worship at one of our denomination's seminaries. Neither of these roles makes me an expert in Indigenous-settler relationships. These roles do, however, prepare me to be a student of history and an encourager for other preachers, teachers, and worship leaders. At first, I was reluctant to address this topic. As a settler, how can I possibly begin to address the topic of reconciliation? However, it was made clear to me by an Indigenous woman (Thundering Eagle Woman) that it is the burden and task of the settler to do the work of conciling/reconciling with those we have damaged. Decolonizing the mind is as much a task for the colonizer as it is for the colonized.

I come to this book as someone who is still learning, but I am willing to share what I am discovering along the way. In order to ensure that this process of writing this book was as open and collaborative as possible, I invited a team of individuals—Indigenous and settler—to walk with me,

48. Travis, *Decolonizing Preaching*, 128.

challenging and encouraging the writing of this book. Their wisdom is frequently found within these pages, and I consider them to be coauthors. Margaret Mullin, Brian Fraser, Germaine Lovelace, and Lori Ransom have been faithful companions on this journey. Margaret identifies as Irish-Ojibway, Brian as a Scottish Canadian settler, Germaine as an Afro-Caribbean settler in Canada, and Lori as a mix of Indigenous (Algonquin) and settler. The task of reconciling is not a lone-ranger task—it is enacted in community.

I have committed to highlighting Indigenous voices, although I realize that in doing so I still possess the power to choose which voices are heard and how clearly. I am writing from the perspective of a white settler, born in Canada, privileged in every way. I am inspired by a desire to participate in healing and reconciliation as a settler who deeply benefits from the oppression of Indigenous peoples. My paternal grandfather worked for the Hudson's Bay Company in the early part of the twentieth century, a company which participated in colonizing the lands that we now call Canada. My denomination was a willing participant in residential schools and continues to struggle to enact relationship with those they have harmed. I live on lands that have been stolen from Indigenous peoples. My partner works for a Canadian railway, which has its own history of colonization and dereliction. Canada's political, judicial, education, medical, and other social systems privilege "people like me" over those who are Indigenous, and the consequences for Indigenous peoples are severe. I write with an awareness of all of these things, hopeful that my words will go a small way toward acknowledging, even healing, the divide.

This is not a book about incorporating Indigenous spiritual practices, such as smudging, into Christian worship. While these are valid and life-giving practices, I believe that they should be incorporated into Christian worship only with the express approval and guidance of Indigenous Elders and Knowledge Keepers. I do, however, rely on themes of Indigenous spirituality and the spiritual wisdom of Indigenous guides. These offer a profound critique of some reformed worship practices and underlying theologies. I operate according to the perspective of traditioned innovation. "Traditioned innovation is a way of moving into the future with a creative and hopeful spirit while respecting and bringing forward the best of an institution's history. Innovating within one's tradition provides a foundation of faith, familiarity and knowledge on which institutions and their leaders can experiment and improvise their way into a Holy Spirit-inspired future."[49] My hope is to offer some theological bases and liturgical tools to aid

---

49. White, "Hope of Traditioned Innovation," abstract.

preachers and worship leaders to construct worship in such a way that it opens the possibility for reconciliation/conciliation—with God and with others.

I frequently use the term *we* in this book. I am referring to worship leaders who minister in the context of contemporary colonialism, particularly white settlers. This book may be most helpful for white-dominant churches in North America, although I have tried to consider the ways that truth and reconciliation affects newcomers and immigrants. While much of the content is Canadian, the situation of my country is shared by many other settler nations, including the United States. I am hopeful that the Canadian context will serve as a lesson for other nations struggling with Indigenous-settler relations. I am also hopeful that this book will be met with strong critique by Indigenous Christians so that our process of learning may continue.

From a decolonizing perspective, chapter 1 examines the situation of Canadian Protestant churches in terms of their history of relationships with Indigenous people. I define *settler-colonialism* and review the continuing impact of the Doctrine of Discovery on theological traditions. This chapter reflects on worship through the framework of the United Nations Declaration on the Rights of Indigenous Peoples (UNDRIP).

Chapter 2 discusses the imperfection of our worship, the role of reconciliation in worship, and the barriers to conciliation/reconciliation that arise between settler Christians and Indigenous peoples. In what ways does reformed worship need to be decolonized? The next four chapters explore the character of worship within the fourfold structure of reformed worship.

Chapter 3 is centered on the gathering, including land acknowledgments, the significance of confession and pardon, and lament, as well as briefly tracing some of the implications for children's worship and the musical contributions of worship.

Chapter 4 focuses on the word as it is contained in the pages of Scripture. From the passages we choose to read to the manner in which we interpret the gospel, our interaction with the Bible is shaped by colonialism. How do we decolonize our readings of Scripture in a way that facilitates reconciliation with Indigenous peoples? I offer sacred resistance as means of decolonizing scriptural interpretation.

Chapter 5 continues the task of interpreting Scripture through preaching. Attending to the analysis accomplished in chapter 4, this chapter proposes that sermons are a key element in forming congregational attitudes and behaviors. Using a decolonizing lens, I argue for a perspective on the gospel that contextualizes good news. Preaching can transform us into those who have the capacity to engage in conversations about conciliation/

reconciliation. This chapter offers several suggestions and reflects on preaching that addresses residential schools.

Chapter 6 engages the Sacraments and the Prayers of the People. In baptism, we are connected to God and to the whole of creation; we discover our creation story, which grounds us in the work of reconciliation with others and with the earth itself. At the Lord's table, we encounter the challenge of forgiveness given and received by God and by others.

Chapter 7 explores what happens beyond the benediction. We are sent out to actively participate in the task of restorative solidarity. Drawing from the work of Elaine Enns and Ched Myers and Randy S. Woodley, I seek to create a pattern of response to worship that involves deep engagement with Indigenous peoples and the continuing work of decolonizing Christian practice.

Worship leaders will find this book especially helpful if they are struggling to find words and actions that can adequately respond to contemporary situations in which Indigenous people are oppressed and suppressed by the nation-state. Through lament, confession, biblical preaching, sensitive prayer, and jubilant song we encounter the divine. We are also brought near to all those who suffer and struggle. Worship, rooted in God's grace, gives us hope when hope is absent. It reorients us away from superiority and violence toward equity and compassion. May we find words and ways of hope than can transcend this present darkness.

1

THE LIE OF THE LAND

THE CONFESSION OF THE Presbyterian Church in Canada as adopted by the 120th General Assembly, June 9th, 1994 says this:

> The Holy Spirit, speaking in and through Scripture, calls The Presbyterian Church in Canada to confession. This confession is our response to the Word of God. We understand our mission and ministry in new ways in part because of the testimony of Aboriginal peoples.
>
> 1. We, the 120th General Assembly of The Presbyterian Church in Canada, seeking the guidance of the Spirit of God, and aware of our own sin and shortcomings, are called to speak to the Church we love. We do this, out of new understandings of our past not out of any sense of being superior to those who have gone before us, nor out of any sense that we would have done things differently in the same context. It is with humility and in great sorrow that we come before God and our Aboriginal brothers and sisters with our confession.
>
> 2. We acknowledge that the stated policy of the Government of Canada was to assimilate Aboriginal peoples to the dominant culture, and that The Presbyterian Church in Canada co-operated in this policy. We acknowledge that the roots of the harm we have done are found in the attitudes and values of western European colonialism, and the assumption that what was not yet moulded in our image was to be discovered and exploited. As part of that policy we, with other churches, encouraged the government to ban some important spiritual

practices through which Aboriginal peoples experienced the
presence of the creator God. For the Church's complicity in
this policy we ask forgiveness.

3. We recognize that there were many members of The Presbyterian Church in Canada who, in good faith, gave unstinting-
ly of themselves in love and compassion for their Aboriginal
brothers and sisters. We acknowledge their devotion and
commend them for their work. We recognize that there
were some who, with prophetic insight, were aware of the
damage that was being done and protested, but their efforts
were thwarted. We acknowledge their insight. For the times
we did not support them adequately nor hear their cries for
justice, we ask forgiveness.

4. We confess that The Presbyterian Church in Canada pre-
sumed to know better than Aboriginal peoples what was
needed for life. The Church said of our Aboriginal brothers and sisters, "If they could be like us, if they could think
like us, talk like us, worship like us, sing like us, and work
like us, they would know God and therefore would have life
abundant." In our cultural arrogance we have been blind to
the ways in which our own understanding of the Gospel has
been culturally conditioned, and because of our insensitivity to Aboriginal cultures, we have demanded more of the
Aboriginal people than the Gospel requires, and have thus
misrepresented Jesus Christ who loves all peoples with compassionate, suffering love that all may come to God through
him. For the Church's presumption we ask forgiveness.

5. We confess that, with the encouragement and assistance of
the Government of Canada, The Presbyterian Church in
Canada agreed to take the children of Aboriginal peoples
from their own homes and place them in residential schools.
In these schools, children were deprived of their traditional
ways, which were replaced with Euro-Canadian customs that
were helpful in the process of assimilation. To carry out this
process, The Presbyterian Church in Canada used disciplin-
ary practices which were foreign to Aboriginal peoples, and
open to exploitation in physical and psychological punishment beyond any Christian maxim of care and discipline. In
a setting of obedience and acquiescence there was opportunity for sexual abuse, and some were so abused. The effect
of all this, for Aboriginal peoples, was the loss of cultural

identity and the loss of a secure sense of self. For the Church's insensitivity we ask forgiveness.

6. We regret that there are those whose lives have been deeply scarred by the effects of the mission and ministry of The Presbyterian Church in Canada. For our Church we ask forgiveness of God. It is our prayer that God, who is merciful, will guide us in compassionate ways towards helping them to heal.

7. We ask, also, for forgiveness from Aboriginal peoples. What we have heard we acknowledge. It is our hope that those whom we have wronged with a hurt too deep for telling will accept what we have to say. With God's guidance our Church will seek opportunities to walk with Aboriginal peoples to find healing and wholeness together as God's people.[1]

I did not learn about residential schools as a child. While the school curriculum included Indigenous settlement patterns and traditional ways of life, it was always from the perspective of the white settler. I recall reading about the bison and how they were hunted, and how all their parts were used by "native" people. There was no mention of hardship or abuse, no telling the stories of the children who never came home. There was no mention of stolen land. Instead, we heard about "explorers" and pioneers who traveled benignly from afar in order to settle an empty land. Once in Canada, these explorers and pioneers were supported and helped by the friendly tribes of Indigenous folk. That is the story I learned.

It wasn't until I was almost an adult, attending the 1994 General Assembly of the Presbyterian Church in Canada as a Young Adult Representative, that I was exposed to a darker aspect of my country's history.[2] The 1994 General Assembly of the PCC offered a confession that outlined its misdeeds and sinfulness in relation to Indigenous peoples. It was the first time I heard of residential schools or had any idea that the church had been

---

1. The Confession of the Presbyterian Church in Canada was presented to Mr. Phil Fontaine, then Grand Chief of the Assembly of Manitoba Chiefs, on October 8, 1994, at The Forks in Winnipeg, Manitoba, by the moderator of the 120th General Assembly, the Rev. Dr. George Vais, and former president of the Women's Missionary Society, Mrs. Kay Cowper. On the twentieth anniversary of the Confession in 2014, it was again presented to Mr. Phil Fontaine, this time translated into multiple Indigenous languages. Mr. Fontaine acknowledged the confession as a "special moment between the PCC and indigenous peoples" and as setting the stage for a journey that we embark on together. "On this journey we have to walk together," he said. "We no longer live in an isolated world apart from one another; we are very much together."

2. The PCC is a mainline denomination in Canada with approximately one thousand worshiping congregations. As a denomination, it belongs to the reformed tradition.

involved in such a destructive project. It was my first hint that relationships between white people and Indigenous people were not good. Thinking back, I wonder how I failed to comprehend the significance of events like the Oka crisis; and yet, I was very young and these events were not discussed in school.[3] I remember being moved by the Presbyterian confession, thinking that it was good to say sorry, without having any personal understanding for what exactly we were apologizing. I was just finishing high school at the time, learning about the TRC process in South Africa, without having any understanding of what would be required within my own country. The confession left a mark on me, and yet I would go through seminary in a PCC institution and earn a doctorate from the same institution without furthering my education about Indigenous-settler relations. It was simply not part of the curriculum, at least not in any memorable way. So there I was, an ordained minister teaching in a theological college of the PCC without a deep grounding in reconciliation. Without a grasp of the significance of the poverty of relationship among settlers and Indigenous peoples and why that mattered to the church and to the society. It was only after the TRC Calls to Action were published that I began to ask questions about the role of the church in reconciliation.

My experience is not unique. When children's graves were uncovered in the spring of 2021, many Canadians were shocked and horrified by the very existence of residential schools that had not, until that point, been part of public awareness. Some had trouble believing that the news was true—after all, the ill-treatment of Indigenous communities is not in alignment with Canadian self-understanding. Preferring to view ourselves as a peaceful and beneficent nation, it is a terrible shock to come to terms with a history that tells an opposite story. This lack of knowledge or acknowledgment reflects a significant gap in the historical education of children and adults. While Canadian children today do learn about residential schools and have access to an array of helpful materials for learning about Canada's history of oppression and genocide, there remains an educational gap within the church. Almost thirty years after the Confession, my denomination still struggles to

---

3. On the morning of July 11, 1990, officers of the Sûreté du Québec attempted a raid on armed Kanehsatake Mohawk land defenders blockading the site of a proposed golf course expansion on their territory (coincident with the town of Oka, Quebec). The expansion was unpopular among both Mohawks and settler residents of Oka, who cited environmental concerns over soil erosion. After a long summer of police and military escalation, settler terrorism and incessant media coverage, land defenders found themselves cornered by the Army and chose, discordantly, to disengage. Some Indigenous people credit the crisis with providing a renewed sense of national agency and pride, and it has been linked to the consolidation of Nunavut as an independently governed Inuit territory. See York, *People of the Pines*.

live by it. Most Presbyterians are not educated about the church's role in residential schools or the theological imperative for conciliation/reconciliation.

Worship prepares us for the work of conciliation/reconciliation. Through God's action in story and prayer, song and silence we are educated and inspired toward deeper relationship with one another. Worship leaders may find themselves in a similar situation to that which I have described above—lacking knowledge about Indigenous affairs and the relationship of settler Christians to Indigenous peoples. If we are serious about the project of decolonizing worship, we will need to educate ourselves and our congregations. If we are to narrate the truth, we must possess information about Indigenous-settler relationships and the true stories of our nations. These are massive stories that span decades and enormous territories and incorporate millions of people. In a brief chapter, it is not possible to even begin to summarize Indigenous-settler relationships in North America. This chapter instead offers some tools and definitions that will aid the worship leader in crafting worship services that are sensitive and attentive to themes of reconciliation. I will define *settler-colonialism* with reference to the Canadian experience and consider the historical function of the Doctrine of Discovery. I will also examine the United Nations Declaration on the Rights of Indigenous Peoples (UNDRIP) in light of how the declaration "unsettles" the liturgy of the church.

Thirty years after a landmark confession, the Presbyterian Church in Canada, like most denominations, struggles to live out the promises implied in its words. These are promises to do better, to avoid the mistakes made by past generations, to listen and be attentive to the voices that have been silenced historically. The PCC asked forgiveness from God and from Indigenous people for residential schools and the harm perpetuated there. The harm is not merely historical but reaches its tentacles through time and space and causes damage in the present. The harm continues to unfold within Indigenous communities, and the church—the whole church—must be held accountable for its past and present failures, which it has expressed in its own confessions. It is disheartening to be reminded that time does not equal progress and that the work of conciliation/reconciliation is not straightforward but a very long and complicated process.

As we confess the ongoing realities of white supremacy and colonialism, we are reminded that the God to whom we confess is also the God who is able to transform people and situations. Worship reminds us that the very worst we have to offer is met by God's very best. Even as we encounter a laundry list of human sins in relation to Indigenous peoples, we are surprised by grace and the hope that a new community will arise. Let us turn to defining some of the key terms and concepts that lay a foundation for the conversations in this book.

Settler Colonialism

I have always lived within a four hundred kilometer (250 mile) radius in southern Ontario. While I have travelled widely, my identity is tied to particular places in the most southern part of Canada. My parents were born and raised within the same radius. I have very little understanding of how my family came to be on this land. It was simply not a topic of discussion in my household—we did not think about our origin stories or where we came from. Perhaps because our family has been in Canada for several generations we have lost any connection to other lands. Neither did we talk about the land on which we lived. Ours was a very urban/suburban existence, far away from the produce and harvest. I knew from school about the patterns of settlement in the area, but the topic of whose land it was to begin with never came up. I simply belonged in the place where I was born, my family owned its modest bit of land, and it never occurred to me to wonder about my own identity in relation to the land. I suspect it is a different experience for farming families or those living in smaller communities. My experience is certainly not reflective of most Canadians, whose memories of home mix with hopes for a future in a new place. We are a nation of immigrants: Most of us have come from elsewhere. There are Indigenous communities, however, who have been here longer than anyone else: The original inhabitants of the land, who have borne responsibility for stewarding creation in these regions for thousands of years.

When we worship, we bring our whole selves. We bring the various roles and identities that constitute self. The divine invites us into relationship as we are, not in some perfect imitation of goodness but in the ordinariness of our imperfection. Thus, we come as daughters and sons, partners, parents, workers, spiritual beings, neighbors, members of ethnic groups, sexual beings—all the various identities that make us who we are. These identities will affect how we hear and understand the word of God, how we encounter others in the worship space, our comforts and discomforts related to liturgy. There is another kind of identity that forms the worshiping self—our identity in relation to the land. I come to worship as a settler. Why does my identity as a settler matter in the worship space? This identity will impact how I understand God's nature and action. It will impact how I understand myself in relation to creation. It will impact my relationship to God and other people, especially Indigenous people.

Part of the commitment to conciliation/reconciliation is to think carefully about identities in relation to the land. The 1994 Confession, for example, links Presbyterian identity to colonialism. If we are to move toward right relations, it becomes necessary for settlers to identify themselves as such. This is not to assume that everyone is comfortable with the term *settler*. The point is that insofar as we are wanting to enter into genuine dialogue about conciliation/reconciliation, we who are not Indigenous need to come to terms with the fact that we are occupying land that does not belong to us. The following section takes a closer look at settler colonialism and what it means to be a settler Christian living in North America.

Settler colonialism has three main pillars, according to Barker and Lowman. The first is that the settlers come into possession of the land by invasion.[4] Invasion, in this case, is a structure rather than an event—invasion is not only a past action but a continuing reality because the economic, political, and social structures of invasion remain.[5] Secondly, settlers come to stay—they are not temporary visitors but plan to settle down into life on the land they have invaded. This makes them different, in many cases, from colonial administrators, traders, and soldiers whose stay is intended to be temporary.[6] "A settler society is created when a newcomer people shift from identifying with the distant empires and states that often founded them and from which they emigrated, to identify primarily with the political constructs, goals and society in a new homeland."[7] Settlers who plan to remain in the land need to develop justifications for why they can consider themselves to be "at home" on land that belongs to others.

Thirdly, the end goal of settler colonialism is to transcend colonialism—to eliminate Indigenous peoples and deeply establish setters as the natural, normal, unquestioned, unchallenged inhabitants of the land.[8] Settler histories are whitewashed to avoid any suggestion that the settler's presence should be challenged.

Settler colonialism is rooted in the Doctrine of Discovery, a "legal fiction" by which Europeans claimed Indigenous lands for themselves.[9] Mark Charles, a Diné scholar, tells of coming upon a Columbus Day ceremony in Washington, DC, that was celebrating the "discovery" of America. His response to this group was to say, "You cannot discover lands already

---

4. Lowman and Barker, *Settler*, 25.
5. Lowman and Barker, *Settler*, 25.
6. Lowman and Barker, *Settler*, 25.
7. Lowman and Barker, *Settler*, 27.
8. Lowman and Barker, *Settler*, 26.
9. Manuel et al., *Unsettling Canada*, 3.

inhabited. That process is known as stealing, conquering, or colonizing. The fact that America calls what Columbus did 'discovery' reveals the implicit racial bias of the country—that Native Americans are not fully human."[10] However, this idea of discovery is deeply rooted in the historical doctrines of the church. The Doctrine of Discovery is "a set of legal principles that governed the European colonizing powers, particularly regarding the administration of indigenous land."[11] It became the justification for colonization, as Indigenous peoples were seen as the enemies of God and white Europeans were viewed as the rightful owners of the land and innately superior to its original inhabitants. This white supremacy has persisted to this day and has been confirmed by the adherence of Christian entities to the Doctrine of Discovery. As the World Council of Churches states in its "Statement on the Doctrine of Discovery and Its Enduring Impact on Indigenous Peoples":

> Consequently, the current situation of Indigenous Peoples around the world is the result of a linear programme of "legal" precedent, originating with the Doctrine of Discovery and codified in contemporary national laws and policies. The Doctrine mandated Christian European countries to attack, enslave and kill the Indigenous Peoples they encountered and to acquire all of their assets. The Doctrine remains the law in various ways in almost all settler societies around the world today. The enormity of the application of this law and the theft of the rights and assets of Indigenous Peoples have led indigenous activists to work to educate the world about this situation and to galvanize opposition to the Doctrine. Many Christian churches that have studied the pernicious Doctrine have repudiated it, and are working to ameliorate the legal, economic and social effects of this international framework.[12]

Upon arriving in the lands that are now called North America, Europeans viewed these lands as *Terra Nullius*—empty lands that were waiting to be occupied by benevolent nations that would settle and civilize the land. Initially, the European traders and Indigenous peoples had more or less friendly relations,

> but gradually, the numbers of these uninvited guests began to increase, and they began to act less and less like guests and more and more as lords. It was a process that Indigenous peoples around the world have experienced. The strangers arrive and

10. Charles and Rah, *Unsettling Truths*, loc. 208.

11. Charles and Rah, *Unsettling Truths*, loc. 220.

12. World Council of Churches, "Statement on the Doctrine of Discovery."

offer trade and friendship. The Indigenous population responds
in kind. Gradually the strangers begin to take up more and more
space and make more and more requests from their hosts, until
finally they are not requesting at all. They are demanding. And
they are backing up their demands with garrisoned outposts.[13]

Barker and Lowman describe the process by which this occurs: "As Indigenous peoples are physically and conceptually displaced, settler society grows
into the (perceived) open space created by their (perceived) absence."[14]

The land was acquired forcefully and without permission, relegating
Indigenous populations to reserves. Seldom were these small parcels of land
able to sustain Indigenous ways of life, leading to poverty and a distinct
lack of well-being in many areas of life. Some of the movement of Indigenous peoples in North America has been determined by the negotiation
of treaties, which in Indigenous perspective "are long-term frameworks for
equitable relationships rather than documents detailing land surrender or
political alliance-making."[15] Treaties are designed to allow settler people to
live on the land "in a more ethical and legitimate fashion."[16] Treaties were
frequently negotiated in an unfair manner, broken, or ignored, rather than
being symbols of trust and mutual respect.[17]

The explicit racism within Canadian history is mind boggling, and
the goal was to continue "until there is not a single Indian in Canada that
has not been absorbed."[18] The assumption was that Indigenous populations could be exterminated, and those that remained would be civilized
and Christianized without regard for their own rich cultures. Even once
Indigenous people were granted the right to vote without disavowing their
heritage, many were reluctant to vote, not seeing themselves as Canadians
but "as members of sovereign nations trapped inside a country that they
had never sought to be a part of."[19] The residential school system was part of
the "solution" to the "problem" of Indigenous peoples' continued existence.
By removing children from Indigenous communities, they were distanced
from (and forbidden to practice) their languages and cultures.

---

13. Manuel et al., *Unsettling Canada*, 4.

14. Lowman and Barker, *Settler*, 27.

15. Lowman and Barker, *Settler*, 65.

16. Lowman and Barker, *Settler*, 66.

17. Lowman and Barker, *Settler*, 65.

18. Titley, *Narrow Vision*, 50, cited in Manuel et al., *Unsettling Canada*, 9.

19. Manuel et al., *Unsettling Canada*, 24.

Land is at the center of Indigenous-settler relations and perhaps constitutes the key difference between Indigenous and settler identities.[20] Settlers continue to claim ownership of the land regardless of the degree of colonial violence with which it was seized. The title of this chapter, "The Lie of the Land," is intended as a double entendre that calls our attention to the reality that the lands of North America were illegally acquired with enormously negative consequences for Indigenous populations. Amid the origin stories of settlers in North America, it is important to acknowledge that these colonial histories have become the colonial present.

As Arthur Manuel writes, "It is the loss of our land that has been the precise cause of our impoverishment."[21] Today in Canada, Indigenous peoples control only 0.2 percent of the land.[22] In addition to the consequences of poverty, "our lives are seven years shorter than the lives of non-Indigenous Canadians. Our unemployment rates are four times higher. The resources to educate our children are only a third of what is spent on non-Indigenous children. Our youth commit suicide at a rate more than five times higher. We are living the effects of this dispossession every day of our lives, and we have been living this misery in Canada for almost 150 years."[23]

Despite all of these barriers, despite the ongoing manifestations of settler colonialism, Indigenous peoples have survived and thrived. It is important to perceive the diversity and beauty of Indigenous ways of life and to honor the ways that survivors have been able to integrate their experience, resist oppression, and work to nurture and sustain their own communities. While tragedy abounds, so does resilience and empowerment. With intergenerational trauma comes intergenerational wisdom. In their work that describes the economic development of Indigenous communities, Stephen Cornell and Joseph Kalt argue:

> What much of the world doesn't know is that in the last quarter century, a number of those nations have broken away from the prevailing pattern of poverty. They have moved aggressively to take control of their futures and rebuild their nations, rewriting constitutions, reshaping economies, and reinvigorating indigenous community and culture. Today, they are creating sustainable, self-determined economies and building societies that work.[24]

20. Lowman and Barker, *Settler*, 18.

21. Manuel et al., *Unsettling Canada*, 7.

22. Manuel et al., *Unsettling Canada*, 8.

23. Manuel et al., *Unsettling Canada*, 8.

24. Cornell and Kalt, "Two Approaches to the Development," 6.

We should never underestimate the ability of Indigenous communities to self-govern, to respond powerfully to settler oppression, and to create a life-sustaining vision not only for themselves but for all who dwell in the land. Paulette Regan writes of a "rich counter-narrative" that has been enacted by Indigenous peoples across Turtle Island (North America).[25] This is a narrative of resistance to colonialism, which seeks to reclaim Indigenous histories and cultures, including the reclamation of languages, governance, and legal systems.[26]

Living as Settler-Dominant Churches

Governments and churches have been preoccupied for generations with solving the "problem" of Indigenous peoples. Historian Roger Epp asks a different question: "How do we solve the settler problem?"[27] This will involve turning the mirror on ourselves as settlers, looking at our actions, attitudes, and responses to the theft of Indigenous land and the oppression of Indigenous cultures. In effect, we are trying to solve problematic settler behavior and attitudes instead of trying to "fix" Indigenous issues. Rather than thinking that we as settlers know what's best for Indigenous peoples, we must determine what needs to change within the settler. Regan wonders about the particular roles and responsibilities of settler people if they are to join survivors on a journey of healing from residential schools as well as all the other consequences of colonial violence.[28] Here, it is useful to ask about the specific roles and responsibilities of settler Christians. Barker and Lowman note that settler and Indigenous identities are always in relationship—they exist in tension with each other and overlap insofar as many people are caught between settler and Indigenous identities. These relationships are complex and involve constant interactions; therefore, the actions of one will impact the other.[29] Thus, the choices we make as settlers have a significant impact on Indigenous peoples. The choices to reject colonial violence, to respond to the Calls to Action from the Truth and Reconciliation Commission, and to reject the Doctrine of Discovery should have a positive effect on the relationships between settlers and Indigenous peoples. Many churches have already rejected the Doctrine of Discovery, recognizing it as a

25. Regan, *Unsettling the Settler*, 3.

26. Regan, *Unsettling the Settler*, 3.

27. Epp, "We Are all Treaty People," 228, cited in Regan, *Unsettling the Settler*, 11. See also Barker and Lowman, *Settler*, 13.

28. Regan, *Unsettling the Settler*, 2.

29. Lowman and Barker, *Settler*, 17.

deeply flawed belief system that places whiteness at the center and relegates everyone else to the margins. For centuries, Indigenous peoples have been forced to adapt to or accommodate settler practices in order to survive. If we are to live respectfully together on the land, settlers "need to take up the responsibility of learning about Indigenous ontologies."[30] By learning about Indigenous ways of knowing, settlers may be able to relate to Indigenous communities in a non-dominating, nonhierarchical way. Settler Christians are prone to a particular kind of domination, which is also known as "benevolent paternalism." In this worldview, colonization has been a peaceful and benevolent effort aimed at the improvement of Indigenous lives, which could not be civilized without the "help" of settlers. Residential schools are a clear example: settlers genuinely believed that they were doing what was best for Indigenous children—that it was better for them to be removed from their homes in order to receive Christian care. Obviously and horrifically, this belief was proved to be absolutely incorrect, and resulted in death, destruction, and trauma for Indigenous peoples.[31]

Settler Christians have the role of mitigating the harm of ongoing colonialism, encouraging Indigenous efforts, and dismantling colonial structures of invasion.[32] It is only through engagement with Indigenous ways of knowing that we will be able to perform these roles and responsibilities. Decolonization is a story, one that settlers are not used to telling. It will take listening, learning, and practice to be able to narrate a different story about our future on the land, one that honors Indigenous occupants and makes space for the negotiation of colonial identity.

Implications for Worship

The following chapters will outline the implications of worshiping as settlers in a context of inequitable, broken relationships with Indigenous peoples. I will explore settler identity further in chapter 7, but for now it is important to recognize that we "show up" in the worship space as settlers. We come with relative power, especially those of us who are white and whose families have long lived on the land. There are, of course, varying degrees of power and influence among settlers, and settler privilege may be limited for immigrants or people of color whose ancestors were enslaved. For example, what is the experience of immigrants who have come later to the land, for whom settler identity is not a good fit? People of color have often endured

30. Lowman and Barker, *Settler*, 20.

31. Not every child had a negative experience at residential schools.

32. Lowman and Barker, *Settler*, 120.

colonial violence in their homelands and in their adopted countries. As full participants in the life of the land in which they dwell, immigrants may unintentionally contribute to the oppression of Indigenous peoples. The task of decolonizing and the work of conciliation/reconciliation belongs to all who gather for worship regardless of their colonial status and experience. As noted frequently throughout this book, all are caught in systems of violence and oppression, generally without their permission. Settlers, immigrants, Indigenous peoples—all are needed in order to have this conversation about how churches will approach the concept of conciliation/reconciliation.

Given the absolute centrality of the land in the relationship between settlers and Indigenous peoples, churches will need to wrestle with their own ownership and stewardship of the land. We meet for worship in a particular location that has a particular history. We have a responsibility to this land and to others who have inhabited it. Chapter 3 will discuss the acknowledgment of the land as a component of settler worship; however, it is valuable for congregations and denominations to think through the manner in which they came to be in possession of the real estate on which churches are built. As denominations shrink, there is land that is no longer required for congregational activity. What will happen to this land as congregations close, and might that land be reallocated to Indigenous peoples?

UNDRIP and the Worship Life of the Church: A Reflection

The United Nations Declaration on the Rights of Indigenous Peoples (UNDRIP) is a living document that was adopted by the UN in 2007. It outlines the rights of Indigenous persons throughout the world. It affirms the equality of all people, specifically naming the fact that Indigenous peoples are equal to all other peoples and contribute richly to our shared life. People are equal but different, and while those differences matter, no group is superior to another. "All doctrines, policies and practices based on or advocating superiority of peoples or individuals on the basis of national origin or racial, religious, ethnic or cultural differences are racist, scientifically false, legally invalid, morally condemnable and socially unjust."[33] The statement asserts that because of colonization, Indigenous peoples have not been able to exercise their rights, especially their right to development of their own communities. Indigenous peoples, however, have worked to respond to colonization, and have created social, economic, cultural, and political structures that allow them to flourish. It is important that Indigenous people maintain control of their lands and resources and all decisions

33. United Nations, UNDRIP, 3.

related to them. The statement takes into consideration the treaties and agreements that have been created between Indigenous peoples and states, wishing those treaties and agreements to be honored by all parties. Particularly poignant is the reminder that Indigenous peoples have a right to raise their children according to the customs and norms of their communities. UNDRIP recognizes and reaffirms "that Indigenous individuals are entitled without discrimination to all human rights recognized in international law, and that Indigenous peoples possess collective rights which are indispensable for their existence, well-being and integral development as peoples."[34] It also affirms the great diversity among Indigenous groups and that the particularities and uniqueness of each should be taken into consideration.

This is a valuable document, and its forty-six articles outline how the rights of Indigenous peoples globally may be exercised and preserved. It is incumbent upon settler states who have signed this declaration to honor the rights of Indigenous peoples who share the land with us, as well as those in other lands far and near. UNDRIP should be a wake-up call for the church, and we must ask ourselves about the ways in which we can honor the declaration in our shared life as the body of Christ.[35] "If Canadian churches follow through on this commitment, it will introduce fundamental changes into their relationships to Indigenous Peoples. Consultation with Indigenous Peoples, acknowledgement of their rights, respect for their traditions, practices, and teachings will have to become standard practice for Canadian churches."[36] UNDRIP is

> fundamentally a call for settler societies to manifest a new love and respect for Indigenous Peoples. To speak for a moment in Christian terms, the churches are realizing that the Holy Spirit has addressed them through the movement that gave rise to the Declaration, calling them to respect Indigenous Peoples and their cultures, practices, traditions, religions, and lands. The Declaration codifies what this means in the language of human rights at this point in time.[37]

34. United Nations, UNDRIP, 7.

35. In 2016, seven Canadian churches issued "An Ecumenical Statement on the United Nations Declaration on the Rights of Indigenous Peoples." This statement was rooted in the Calls to Action that emerged from the Truth and Reconciliation Commission, specifically number forty-eight, which is a mandate to formally adopt and comply with the principles, norms, and standards of the UNDRIP as a framework for reconciliation. See Kairos, "Ecumenical Statement." See also Schweitzer and Gareau, *Honouring the Declaration*, 33.

36. Schweitzer and Gareau, *Honouring the Declaration*, 16.

37. Schweitzer and Gareau, *Honouring the Declaration*, 18.

As churches, we worship with the well-being of others in mind. Nothing in worship should detract from what is stated in the Declaration. Instead, our worship should honor the rights of Indigenous peoples in terms of self-determination, their contributions to the lands in which they live, and the beauty and diversity of Indigenous populations. Worship that honors the declaration will avoid any type of "spiritual violence," which has been defined by the Canadian Truth and Reconciliation Commission in light of the residential school system and occurs when "a person's spiritual or religious tradition, beliefs, or practices are demeaned or belittled."[38] How might this "spiritual violence" occur within the space of worship? Any time that colonial narratives sneak into our worship through our prayers, preaching, interpretation of Scripture, or hymns, or if we fail to acknowledge that the land is not our own, we are potentially committing spiritual violence. A form of spiritual violence occurs when we appropriate Indigenous practices that do not belong to us as settlers. It is valuable, of course, to learn from Indigenous ways of knowing, but we must be careful to avoid cultural appropriation. In order to create spiritually nourishing worship, we must remember that we worship in a context of settler colonialism and that such colonialism must be expunged from our worship practices. This book is, in part, a response to the question of how worship may be decolonized so that it fully honors the rights of Indigenous peoples. Until those rights are honored and prioritized by the church, conciliation/reconciliation remains beyond our grasp.

Worship that can prepare us for the sacred work of building relationship must respect Indigenous peoples as equal conversation partners. It must confess and apologize for the wrongs that have been committed by Christians. It must work toward a new vision of community that is motivated by a commitment to equality and justice. Settler Christians, as they come to worship, will remember that there are many Indigenous members of this body of Christ, with whom we share, at least in spirit, the gifts of water, wine, and bread. In worship we are bound to our Indigenous siblings. Thus, our worship should be structured in such a way that it includes and welcomes Indigenous Christians. I argue that worship prepares us to engage with others beyond the worship space, including non-Christian Indigenous communities. The following chapters answer the question, How is worship to be decolonized so that it prepares us for the challenging work of relationship building with those we have harmed?

38. Schweitzer and Gareau, *Honouring the Declaration*, 52. See also Truth and Reconciliation Commission, *Canada's Residential Schools*, 6:96–98.

2

AN IMPERFECT OFFERING
Worship and Barriers to Conciliation

I WAS TAUGHT THAT when presiding at a communion service, I bear responsibility to ensure that everything flows gracefully—perfectly. There should be no awkwardness, no stumbling over invitations or prayers. The silver should be shiny, the cloth should be white, and all should be elegant. On a warm August morning, I was serving communion to my congregation. During the Great Prayer of Thanksgiving, I noticed a commotion in the balcony of the sanctuary. People seemed agitated, ducking their heads. Then I noticed the bat circulating and terrorizing these unfortunate communion-receivers. The peace of the sacrament was shattered as the bat dive-bombed the congregation. Joking about the presence of the Holy Spirit symbolized by the bat, we went on to share the sacrament. This was a reminder that worship does not always go according to plan. It is an imperfect offering. While my story about the bat is entertaining, it does not capture the full implications of this imperfection. Our worship is imperfect when it fails to include a multitude of others. It is imperfect when it doesn't expand its bounds to embrace the hurting and the marginalized. It is imperfect when it ignores the ways that the gospel has been twisted and abused in order to demonize or ignore Indigenous peoples. It is imperfect when we as leaders encourage uncritical adoption of church doctrine without acknowledging our complicity in the settler nation-state.

We come to worship with our histories and personalities intact. We do not leave our trauma, biases, assumptions, or misconceptions at the door of the sanctuary. Rather, these things shape our participation in worship—the manner in which we listen, hear, and respond to the gospel. We are also human beings with agency. We act in and through our experience of worship to praise, lament, give thanks, interpret, sing, and preach. Worship, of course, begins with God's agency. We gather in response to God's gracious hospitality that invites us to worship despite our imperfections. Worship is an encounter that "wakes us up" so that we can perceive God's action in the world in and through Jesus Christ. The efficacy of worship, however, relies at least in part on our willingness to open our eyes and ears.

As a human endeavor, our worship is always imperfect. Even worship is tainted by the consequences of human sin. "Because nothing created is untouched by the Fall, Christians should not be surprised when lovely and good potentially gracious Christian gestures are damaged, or when human beings deploy those Christian gestures in the perpetuation of damage."[1] Lauren Winner argues that Christians should be able to predict some of the characteristic damages that might be found within our Christian gestures and practices. A doctrine of sin recognizes that our worship is imperfect and prone to mistakes and omissions. A doctrine of providence recognizes that God is working all things for good. In and through worship, God is transforming us, transforming our sin into freedom. Our worship, however, is filled with practices that have a "propensity for violence."[2] This violence occurs when our worship is exclusive, belittling to other traditions, or fails to witness to the image of God in every creature. Feminist authors have critiqued the patriarchal language, actions, and imagery of God that turns a blind eye to the experience of women in worship. Nancy Eiesland has written about the ways that worship foregrounds the experience of able-bodied persons at the cost of full inclusion of disabled persons.[3] The Eucharist, for example, can be a ritual of exclusion and degradation. Andrew Wymer reminds us that liturgy has been a source for domination of particular groups, but it has also been a site of protest and resistance.[4] Wymer writes about the potential for violence in the liturgical space.[5] "If liturgy is to liberate the oppressed, the ideologies and practices of the oppressor must be rejected."[6] As Marjorie Procter-Smith writes, liturgy forms us through rituals "because liturgy (again, like language) shapes us gradually and in tiny increments, words and gestures which are used regularly and repeatedly, although

1. Winner, *Dangers of Christian Practice*, 3.

2. Winner, *Dangers of Christian Practice*, 14.

3. Eiesland, *Disabled God*, 113.

4. Wymer, "Liturgy as Protest," 1–2.

5. Wymer, "Liturgical Intersection of Harm and Healing."

6. Wymer, "Liturgical Intersection of Harm and Healing."

appearing small, have a powerful effect."[7] The language and symbols we use in worship matter, as they gradually shape the community of faith in a particular direction. They may be liberating or oppressive.

Worship is a gift from God that allows us to interact with the divine as a community. We are invited into relationship with God and with each other. Worship is also a gift we offer to God. While considering worship as a gift, we also recognize that, as both givers and receivers of this gift, we are prone to mangling it.[8] Winner argues that the consequences of the fall mean that we receive God's gifts in a damaged way.[9] The Scriptures testify to the damaged way in which people received God's gifts. The gift of creation has been squandered by selfishness and violence. The gift of Jesus Christ was rejected, not only by those who did not believe that Jesus was the Messiah, but even by those who did believe. We receive these perfect gifts in a damaged way because we are damaged.

While worship will be perfect on the other side of the eschaton, in the present day we must accept the gifts of worship with gratitude. Not only with gratitude, argues Winner, but with confession-repentance and lament. When we confess, we name before God the ways in which we have failed to properly receive the gifts we have been offered. When we repent, we turn back toward God who forgives and transforms. We plan to stop doing whatever sinful acts are fuelling our distress and adopt new ways of being. Confession and repentance are both individual and communal acts—we search our private and public and communal lives for the ways that we have received gifts imperfectly. Lament is an appropriate response to damaged gifts and to our mishandling of the gifts. We lament not only for our own small lives but for the damaged cosmos: damage that is beyond our individual responsibility. When we lament, we recognize that it is not possible for human beings to repair the world. Rather, when we lament, we acknowledge that God is the one who repairs. We, however, are invited to participate in that repair.

By examining a community's characteristic damage, it is possible to avert, or avoid altogether, the damaged practice of the gifts. If we are aware, for example, that our tendency is toward anti-Judaism in our Scripture interpretations, we can act to change our interpretations of Scripture in full awareness of the damage our perceptions can cause. If we are aware that our worship perpetuates a particular view of patriarchy and colonization, we can search our practices for spaces where decolonization can flourish. If we

---

7. Procter-Smith, "Reorganizing Victimization," 18.

8. Winner, *Dangers of Christian Practice*, 144.

9. Winner, *Dangers of Christian Practice*, 145.

are aware that our worship works against the goal of truth and reconciliation, we can strategize ways to avoid practices that fail to honor truth and reconciliation and move toward practices that sustain relationships within the church and beyond.

It occurs to me that there is deep beauty even in damaged worship practices. In worship, we gather as our truest selves, bringing with us all of our baggage. We open our mouths to sing, and we are off key. We offer our words of prayer and we stumble. We spill the wine, there are breadcrumbs on the floor, and the child we baptized never shows up again. These are the realities of worship, and yet, something transformative happens in that space. We are prepared for stronger, more intimate relationships. Our mumbled prayers somehow find a place in the heart of someone who is hurting. Our songs are more beautiful because they are in harmony. We are invited into something new, into a life in which we narrate and perform a tribute to the living God. Through an awareness of our imperfect offering, we are brought low, made humble, and hopefully inspired to work toward creating worship practices that are more just, more acceptable, not only to God but also to those with whom we share the earth.

In other words, worship forms us. It forms us to be disciples. The particular ways in which we construct our worship practices will affect the manner in which we live our lives. If our worship constructs us to be superior to other groups of people, then our worship is not forming us for a life of faithfulness. If our worship fails to be inclusive, then our worship is not forming us to go out into the world and embrace those who are different. Thus, worship can potentially form us in negative ways, unless we are attentive to the mismanaged practices. Worship then, is an act of shared discernment in which we examine our hearts and our practices in order to decide what is good and what is not. We examine the flaws and the potential for flaws. We search our worship for practices that serve not as launching pads of grace but as barriers to leading a faithful and generous life.

A Ministry of Reconciliation

As Paul wrote in 2 Corinthians:

> From now on, therefore, we regard no one from a human point of view; even though we once knew Christ from a human point of view, we know him no longer in that way. So if anyone is in Christ, there is a new creation: everything old has passed away; see, everything has become new! All this is from God, who reconciled us to himself through Christ, and has given us the

ministry of reconciliation; that is, in Christ God was reconciling the world to himself, not counting their trespasses against them, and entrusting the message of reconciliation to us. So we are ambassadors for Christ, since God is making his appeal through us; we entreat you on behalf of Christ, be reconciled to God. For our sake he made him to be sin who knew no sin, so that in him we might become the righteousness of God."[10]

Elaine Enns and Ched Myers view this passage as an early New Testament attempt at voicing restorative justice and peacemaking.[11] In worship, we are equipped and prepared for this ministry of reconciliation. First, God has reconciled Godself to us in Jesus Christ. That is the foundation for our worship—that God, Creator, Redeemer, and Sustainer, has come near to us in the person of Jesus Christ, and we respond with joy and thanksgiving, bringing our confessions and laments. In worship, we are urged to be reconciled to God. Yet the story does not end there. Christ has given us this ministry of reconciliation, in which we participate in the reconciling work of God in the world. We come to God as those who are new creations, toiling and hoping for the completion of God's reconciling work. Our role as ambassadors means that we are to demonstrate and enact reconciliation/conciliation within the sanctuary and beyond.

An ambassador, in modern parlance, is generally a high-ranking official, who represents a particular state or government, whose role it is to address another state or government. As "ambassadors of reconciliation," Christians represent not the state but the alternative—the kingdom of God as inaugurated by Jesus Christ.[12] On one hand, this characterization as "ambassadors" is helpful when it applies to the formation of relationships among those understanding themselves to be the people of God. If we are ambassadors of reconciliation, then we are sent out on behalf of God in order to seek reconciliation. Being an ambassador of reconciliation presumes a mutually respectful relationship. On the other hand, Paul's words require some unpacking, especially as they may be used to justify unwanted mission or intrusions into other communities.[13] An ambassador may or may not be welcomed by those for whom the message is intended. If interpreted from a colonial perspective, this passage may presume that it is acceptable to press one's message on another nation without their permission or approval. To

10. 2 Cor 5:16–21.

11. Myers and Enns, *Ambassadors of Reconciliation*, 2.

12. I acknowledge that the term "kingdom of God" is fraught and implies a hierarchical structure that perhaps reflects preferred human hierarchies. I perceive that the kingdom of God operates in stark contrast to the kingdoms of this world.

13. With thanks to Ben Travis-Miller for this insight. Email to author, Dec 6, 2021.

the contrary, to be an ambassador of reconciliation is to approach gently, humbly, and with great respect for the other. Any form of ambassadorship that looks down on the other in a spirit of supremacy, or attempts to force compliance, is not the kind of action which Jesus modeled. All Christians, settler and Indigenous, share this responsibility for facilitating mutually respectful relationships. I do not mean to imply that settler Christians are entirely responsible for this work—rather, a great deal of the burden toward conciliation/reconciliation is shouldered by Indigenous Christians. To position "settlers" as "ambassadors" might suggest that settler Christians are doing this work alone. It is the task of the whole body of Christ (Indigenous and settler), but in reality it has been Indigenous Christians, as well as prophets outside the church, that have pushed for apologies, advocated, and educated others.

We are sent to be in relationship with each other because of the good news in Jesus Christ and God's reconciling movement. The following chapters will look at worship practices, examining them for distortions and danger, as well as the redemptive possibilities of such practices. As we come to worship with our whole selves, we bring the broken pieces as well. What are the barriers to the kind of worship that is able to prepare us for this kind of work? What attitudes and practices do we bring to worship with us that prevent us from being prepared for conciliation/reconciliation?

Settler Fragility and White Fragility

To seek conciliation/reconciliation with others is to enter into a difficult and fraught process. It first requires a deep and honest self-analysis. This is especially challenging when we must confront the topic of race. As the previous chapter reviewed, the relationship between settlers and Indigenous peoples has been complicated and worsened by the racism inherent in settler colonialism. White people hold negative perceptions about Indigenous peoples, often blaming the communities themselves for the hardships they face, downplaying the significance of ongoing colonialism, and claiming a superior position rooted in white supremacy.

In order to prepare ourselves for conciliation/reconciliation, it is helpful to examine ourselves for racist attitudes and behaviors. This process, of course, is not only important for reconciliation with Indigenous peoples. It is also essential work for any congregation that has a mix of races and ethnicities and exists in a multiracial culture. The concepts of white fragility and settler fragility offer insight into the ways that we might seek to protect the category of "whiteness" in order to ease our own cognitive dissonance about the presence of others in the land.

In 2018, American sociologist Robin DiAngelo wrote about the concept of white fragility. Her book rose to the top of the charts following the murder of George Floyd, signalling a recognition that white people need to be accountable for their racial attitudes. *White Fragility* describes the tendency for white people to become uncomfortable when they are confronted with the existence of racism and their own complicity. It can be difficult for individuals to grasp their degree of complicity, especially given a strong and pervasive belief that good people are not racist. On the contrary, even good people can be prone to negative responses when they are made aware of racist attitudes and behaviors.

The concept of white fragility assumes that white people are motivated to maintain their location at the top of a racial hierarchy. All other groups are relegated to "other." "Whiteness rests upon a foundational premise: the definition of whites as the norm or standard for human, and people of color as a deviation from that norm."[14] Encounters that challenge this sense of racial superiority place the white person in a state of racial stress, triggering a number of defensive and self-protective behaviors.[15] These may be outward displays of emotion, such as guilt, fear and anger, argumentation and silence, or leaving the situation altogether. Through these actions, the individual seeks to reduce the racial stress and maintain the equilibrium of white superiority.[16] "Though white fragility is triggered by discomfort and anxiety, it is born of superiority and entitlement."[17] Through our defensiveness, we seek to maintain the racial status quo.[18] DiAngelo claims that these responses prevent us from doing what we should be doing in order to relieve racial tensions—such as "engaging in ongoing self-awareness, continuing education, relationship building and actual anti-racist practice."[19] Even those who consider themselves racially progressive are prone to these habits of response.[20] For example, white Canadians may downplay the negative consequences of residential schools, claiming that "they weren't really that bad" or "they were no worse than any other boarding school." This response functions to protect the white person from feeling bad about themselves

---

14. DiAngelo, *White Fragility*, 25.
15. DiAngelo, *White Fragility*, 1.
16. DiAngelo, *White Fragility*, 103.
17. DiAngelo, *White Fragility*, 2.
18. DiAngelo, *White Fragility*, 3.
19. DiAngelo, *White Fragility*, 5.
20. DiAngelo, *White Fragility*, 5.

and their predecessors, and even their churches, but in doing so they negate the truth of what really happened and avoid taking responsibility for the broken relationships in the present day.

Fragility does not make us "bad" people; it is simply a response to wanting to maintain an identity that we cherish. There is no culturally acceptable way to express our fear that our identity is being destroyed or diminished by the existence of others. "Like a mutating virus, racism shape-shifts in order to stay alive; when its explicit expression becomes taboo, it hides in coded language."[21] It is no surprise that we might experience these things, insofar as we have been supported by a world that reinforces white-ness, the stories of white glorious exploration and colonization, and the distinctions between Black and white people—placing them in a seemingly unalterable hierarchy. Once we have come to terms with the idea of white fragility, DiAngelo claims that we will be in a position of discomfort, which is a desirable key to growth.[22] The goal is to get informed, to become honest with oneself, and to try to build the capacity to endure racial discomfort.

It is important to note that there are some significant critiques of Di-Angelo's perspective. Primarily, DiAngelo seems to recenter whiteness, in that racism becomes all about the feeling and responses of white people. Others have critiqued the lack of quantitative research underlying her ap-proach.[23] DiAngelo also homogenizes whiteness, without accounting for diversity within the white population—surely racial socialization will occur differently depending on culture, ethnicity, and nationality.[24] The theory is very US-centered. My personal critique of DiAngelo arises from the lack of agency I experienced while reading this book. Other than educate myself, how am I supposed to actively engage in anti-racism if I am consistently impacted by my own white fragility? How can we be poised for making positive change if we are encountering fragility at every turn?

Despite these criticisms, DiAngelo's work gives us pause for thought. It caused me to think about my own relationships with members of other racial groups and how I respond to them. How will we as worship leaders, and our congregations, react to the work of decolonization and disrupt-ing racial hierarchies when we are plagued by fragility? I will discuss below some of the responses of the worship leader to white fragility. First, we turn to a related concept: settler fragility.

21. Waldman, "Sociologist Examines the 'White Fragility.'"
22. DiAngelo, *White Fragility*, 142.
23. Waldman, "Sociologist Examines the 'White Fragility.'"
24. Bejan, "Robin DiAngelo's 'White Fragility.'"

Settler fragility arises in the context of settler privilege, which is similar to white privilege in that it is structural, systematic, widespread, and rooted in white supremacy.[25] We are accustomed to "swimming in the water" of the settler state, and thus these waters are considered normative. In terms of the United States, Gilio-Whitaker writes:

> US citizens of all races and ethnic groups have been indoctrinated their entire lives with messages designed to foster a sense of national pride and belonging in the making of what has been called an "imagined community," which always occurs on Indigenous lands. Their citizenship and their very identity are taken for granted without critical consciousness about the US's contradictory foundational structures and narratives.[26]

These structures and narratives are all aimed at the "elimination of the Natives in order to acquire their land, which it does in countless seen and unseen ways. These techniques are woven throughout the US's national discourse at all levels of society. Manifest Destiny—that is, the US's divinely sanctioned inevitability—is like a computer program always operating unnoticeably in the background. In this program, genocide and land dispossession are continually both justified and denied."[27]

The same is true for Canada. Christians in Canada should be aware of the foundational structures and narratives that shape the Canadian experience. We have a view of ourselves as tolerant and welcoming of difference. This "myth of tolerance" means that we sometimes ignore or dismiss the ways in which our culture is not tolerant and welcoming.[28] As a nation of settler colonialism, the goal is often to protect the dominant white population at the expense of others. This unearned privilege is part and parcel of being non-Indigenous. No one wants to be associated with genocide or the destruction of Indigenous lands, and settlers sometimes assume that it makes one a "bad person" to be complicit in these realities. Settler fragility does not rely on the binary of good/bad but assumes that all are caught in a web of complicity. In order to avoid the negative connotations of being a party to "the real and symbolic violences of settler colonialism," settlers employ a set of moves, what scholars Tuck and Yang have called "moves to innocence, moves to comfort."[29] "Settler moves to innocence are those strategies or positionings that attempt to relieve the settler of feelings of

25. Gilio-Whitaker, "Settler Fragility."
26. Gilio-Whitaker, "Settler Fragility."
27. Gilio-Whitaker, "Settler Fragility."
28. Wallis et al., *Colonialism and Racism in Canada*, 2, 7.
29. Tuck and Yang, "Decolonization Is Not a Metaphor," 2.

guilt or responsibility without giving up land or power or privilege, without having to change much at all."[30] In order for settlers to claim the land as home, they must account for the presence of others in the land. This frequently involves "disappearing" Indigenous people from the land by denying or ignoring their presence.[31] Settlers seek ways to become innocent, to disassociate themselves from colonial violence, desiring mercy in the face of relentless guilt.[32]

What is a worship leader to do with the existence of settler and/or white fragility in the worship space? Both serve as barriers to our full and active participation in conciliation/reconciliation. These concepts of fragility help us to understand something about ourselves and our congregants. We are caught in systems of racism from which it is terribly difficult to untangle. It is possible that this whole project of decolonization might be met with alarm and distaste by a community that fears for its own status. Self-awareness is essential for the worship leader in planning and executing worship. Once aware of these fragilities, worship leaders can be prepared for the kinds of responses which might arise within themselves and within their communities. DiAngelo's theory in particular points to the need for education—to become aware of one's own responses and how those responses in fact act as a barrier to cultivating strong relationships with people of different races.

Worship leaders can be prepared for the variety of responses that might arise from within the gathered congregation when referencing issues of conciliation/reconciliation. Some will be seized by guilt and shame for their own complicity in the oppression of Indigenous peoples, emotions that prevent them from entering into genuine reflection and dialogue. Others will become defensive, arguing that colonization was "in the past" and has no bearing on the present. Some will point to the ways that their own cultural group has been marginalized, in an attempt to draw attention away from Indigenous issues. Some will be afraid that the prioritizing of Indigenous rights will detract from their own safety and security on the land. Some will be angry, whether or not they can name it as such. All of these responses, and more, are possible.

By no means does this uncomfortable reality mean that we should avoid talking about conciliation/reconciliation and the consequences of colonialism. Rather, it means that worship leaders must be sensitive and aware. We cannot avoid triggering these emotions and responses. These

30. Tuck and Yang, "Decolonization Is Not a Metaphor," 10.

31. Tuck and Yang, "Decolonization Is Not a Metaphor," 6.

32. Tuck and Yang, "Decolonization Is Not a Metaphor," 9.

fragile responses call for compassion, because those experiencing them are in genuine distress, even if their pain cannot in any sense be compared to the pain of Indigenous peoples or others who have been impacted by racism and oppression.

Worship leaders can address fragile responses by educating our congregations and speaking with care and respect to those who are experiencing fragile responses. However, we must continue to work towards the attitudes and behaviors that will support conciliation/reconciliation. This means that we must name the realities of settler-colonialism and Indigenous oppression. We will hurt some people's feelings. Theologically, this suggests that good news may initially sound more like bad news. For the white person, at first, it may seem like bad news that whiteness is being decentered. It may seem like bad news that resources must be restored to Indigenous communities from whom they were taken in the past. It may seem like bad news to acknowledge the histories and legacies of colonialism. It may seem like bad news that racism is so prevalent, even within those of us who consider ourselves to be "good people." None of this sounds like gospel to the person who is struggling with fragility.

All of this is actually good news, of course. To be decentered is good news, as it makes room for others to dwell in spaces of abundance. To restore resources to Indigenous communities strengthens not only those communities but the ties among human persons. To recognize and honor treaties is to keep the promises made by our ancestors. To acknowledge the histories and legacies of colonialism sets us free from a false narrative, turning us toward a more complete picture of what has been damaged and what might be repaired. The gospel frequently sounds like bad news before it is good news. Death comes before life, drowning comes before rebirth, confession comes before reconciliation.

We resist white fragility and settler fragility by pointing to the hope of a future that is rooted in grace and truth rather than lies and power. It is necessary to walk through the murky aspects of gospel before we can turn to the glorious light. We may journey through guilt, fear, and anger. Untangling these threads of fragility involves a robust gospel that can counteract our negative emotions and responses. The worship leader can name our guilt, fear, and anger out loud, turning them over before our eyes so that we may see the consequences of these emotions.

It is not possible to avoid fragility, but rather to acknowledge and respond to it by holding up the gospel. The gospel promises that what is good news for the marginalized is good news for all. When relationships are strong and vibrant, that is good news for all. When suffering communities have fresh water and resources to educate children, it is good news for all.

When the level of dialogue is increased between settlers and Indigenous communities, it is good news for all. Reconciliation, conciliation, is good news for all. Through the good news of Jesus Christ, our fragilities may be transformed into capacities for renewed relationship.

Trauma

When we come to worship, we bring our whole selves, including our trauma. Our entire culture is traumatized—by division, by violence, by abuse, by faults of nature and our own mistakes. Trauma is a word that means "wound" or "an injury inflicted upon the body by an act of violence."[33] We know that bodily harm need not be present for trauma to exist—it affects the soul and mind as much as the body. Trauma generally involves some sort of threat to personal security. In this age of social media, we have immediate access to the traumatic events that occupy our culture. As I write this, the entire culture is traumatized by COVID-19, not only because of the fear of the disease, but also because of the social unrest that has accompanied the pandemic. We enter the sanctuary with our traumas intact, and these traumas will have an impact on how we participate in and respond to the practices of worship.

Trauma does terrible things to the mind, robbing the individual of agency, imagination, and hope, all of which are essential for the work of conciliation/reconciliation. Trauma creates a barrier to the worship that can equip us for right relations because it stands in the way of our ability to act, imagine, and hope for a different reality.

If we are to enact conciliation/reconciliation, we will require agency—a sense of purpose and responsibility. We will require imagination—to dream beyond the present moment and envision a future in which Indigenous people are enabled to live fully and abundantly. We will require hope—true hope in a living God who is able to overcome even the most hostile divisions. However, trauma stands in the way of these things. Our sense of agency, or how much we feel in control, is determined by the rhythms of our bodies.[34] When we are confident that we are loved and cherished, we are free to say, "This is what I believe in; this is what I stand for; this is what I will devote myself to."[35] In the midst of trauma, however, we may believe that our actions will have no positive consequences, that what we do will make no difference. Individuals dealing with trauma may have more difficulty investing

33. Jones, *Trauma and Grace*, 12.
34. Van der Kolk, *Body Keeps the Score*, 331.
35. Van der Kolk, *Body Keeps the Score*, 350.

themselves in the work of conciliation/reconciliation because they may not believe that any action on their part will make a difference. This is a sense of lethargy. Worship can ground us in the story of God's transformative action, making us participants in a cosmic narrative. By participating in worship by praying, singing, lamenting, and listening, individuals may come to a sense that they are agents in a larger story. God's love is so encompassing that it creates movement within us, which may assist us in reaching toward a larger goal.

In terms of imagination, trauma has been called "a disease of disordered imagination."[36] We might wonder, for example, how a person who has never experienced grace can imagine a gracious response from God or anyone else. God's grace is difficult to grasp—even for those who have experienced it fully, it is a mysterious gift. Imagination is crucial to quality of life, as Bessel van der Kolk writes: "When people are compulsively and constantly pulled back into the past, to the last time they felt intense involvement and deep emotions, they suffer from a failure of imagination, a loss of the mental flexibility. Without imagination there is no hope, no chance to envision a better future, no place to go, no goal to reach."[37] I have proposed that preachers and, in this case, worship leaders act as midwives of the imagination.[38] By riffing on the profound story of God's salvation, the worship leader can guide participants on a journey of imagination, whereby we enter into a new reality that is defined by God's generous future. We assist at the birth of a new song. The old song weaves into the new, for trauma is not forgotten or left behind. In the crevices, however, there is room for imagination to take root.

Worship leaders stand before the congregation, acting as midwives to conciliation/reconciliation. We bear the responsibility and privilege of announcing a new reality, an imagined future in which there is a possibility that what is broken can be restored. In the context of Indigenous-settler relations, we proclaim a new world free from hierarchy and violence. We begin, slowly but surely, to imagine that there is a path forward, that right relationships are a desirable—and possible—outcome of our efforts in partnership with the Holy One. This places an extraordinary burden on the worship leader who must struggle to become free from participation in systematic injustice. Thankfully, the new world we announce is not merely imagined: It is already present in the person of Jesus Christ.

36. Jones, *Trauma and Grace*, 30.
37. Van der Kolk, *Body Keeps the Score*, 17.
38. Travis and Wilson, *Unspeakable*, chapter 4.

It is our hope in God that fuels any movement toward conciliation/ reconciliation. Hope acknowledges that there is a future which will be different from the past, that the same old pattern will not repeat indefinitely. Trauma can immobilize hope, locking us in an eternal past-present loop that plays over and over without the promise of escape. Worship is rooted in hope—the hope of a transformed reality that emerges at the intersection of God's action paired with our modest efforts. In word and sacrament, we live out the hope that God has placed within us. Sometimes, we must hope on behalf of those who cannot hope for themselves. The story of God-with-us is a story that urges hope—that death is not the last word, that there are better orderings of human society, that broken relationships can be made whole.

I have written elsewhere about the tendency of preachers and worship leaders to "rush" to the gospel without leaving adequate room for the reality of trauma.[39] The pain of trauma is unendurable, and no one wants to stay in its shadow. However, if we try to name good news too quickly, we are dishonoring the trauma we carry. Just as we cannot rush to resurrection, neither can we rush to the goal of conciliation/reconciliation. Rather, we sift carefully through the rubble of our emotions and attitudes, turning over traumas and griefs, seeking life amid the ruins.

Indigenous cultures have borne tremendous creativity and spirituality, and yet they are soaked in trauma. In fact, this whole enterprise of truth and reconciliation is steeped in trauma. I am certainly not trying to equate the trauma of settler churches and Indigenous peoples, but simply acknowledging that the topic of truth and reconciliation spawns trauma for both. The history of the people on the land in North America is filled with violence and pain—especially for Indigenous communities. It can, however, be traumatic for settlers to learn about the actions of their ancestors as well as the myriad violences that are perpetrated today against Indigenous peoples. Researching this book was triggering for me as I variously felt grief, guilt, and frustration and was horrified by the truths that have been offered through the Truth and Reconciliation Commission. Working toward conciliation/ reconciliation will inflict at least a hint of trauma on the settler as we are confronted with these realties and the terrible truths that have been told. Trauma cannot be avoided, but it can be honored. Worship leaders can testify to the trauma experienced by those in the pews and by others whom we may or may not know. We can bear witness to the trauma of Indigenous

39. Travis and Wilson, *Unspeakable*, 49.

communities while still being gentle with our own communities. Worship leaders can aid this process by becoming trauma-informed.[40]

Lack of Relationship

Another barrier to worship that can equip us for the work of conciliation/ reconciliation is the lack of relationships between the "white" church and Indigenous Christians. It is difficult to imagine any kind of conciliation/ reconciliation if we are alienated and distanced from those with whom we desire to be in relationship. This is somewhat of a geographical issue. Some churches find themselves in close proximity to Indigenous reserves, and those in urban centers may encounter Indigenous peoples within their own communities. Other churches may not be aware of Indigenous people within the orbit of the congregation, despite their presence. Worship leaders and pastors can reach out to Indigenous organizations in order to create connections and build a foundation for relationships. Churches might encourage worshipers to read books written by Indigenous authors that tell the story of colonialism and its collateral damage. We might engage Indigenous Christian leaders in a conversation that could continue in the worship space during the sermon time. It is in the formation of real relationships that we will be best equipped to enter into conversations about conciliation/ reconciliation.

Western Worldviews

Finally, Western epistemologies and ontologies themselves form barriers to settler ability to acknowledge and respond to damaged relationships. Western perspectives see the autonomous individual as the central unit of meaning in our culture. This can be contrasted with Indigenous worldviews, which place the emphasis on the community. Identity is not found individually but in relation to others. This means that Indigenous communities are perhaps better equipped to address issues of conciliation/reconciliation due to their tendency to interpret the world alongside others rather than relying on individual interpretations. The Western mind places ultimate value on the perspective of the individual rather than on the collective as a meaning-making entity. Paired with an emphasis on the intellect rather than emotion, this individualism means that many of us are ill-equipped to participate in the work of conciliation/reconciliation. Ray Aldred suggests

---

40. See Baldwin, *Trauma-Sensitive Theology*.

that settler brains need to be retrained to tell stories and receive the stories of others using the heart. A patriarchal, Western culture (and, dare I say, the reformed tradition) puts the weight on the mind and intellect, viewing the heart as unreliable and untrustworthy.[41] Settler Christians will benefit from developing an emotional intelligence that will allow us to stop burying emotion. Aldred perceives that churches have no place for those who are half healed.[42] When equipped with emotional intelligence, settlers will be better able to join conversations with Indigenous peoples and to process worship as a project of the heart. This turn to the emotions is necessary if we are to address the trauma that exists both in the sanctuary and in the context of Indigenous-settler relations.

Fragility, trauma, lack of relationship, and Western frameworks are barriers that arise within the worship context. I have shown how worship itself can ameliorate these barriers. The patterns and practices of Christian worship have arisen in a particular context. "If you are a dominant white church or denomination, you have to come to understand that the particular colonization comes out of the history/legacy of Europeans taking over this part of the planet, killing and enslaving millions of people and creating a Christianity that justifies that."[43] Our worship practices and theologies have been formed in the context of domination by groups believing themselves to be culturally superior to Indigenous peoples. Writs such as the Doctrine of Discovery or *Terra Nullis* describe the ways that Christian communities have understood themselves in relation to others. These historical documents, alongside the history of liturgical tradition and theologizing, have shaped the way settlers come to understand worship itself and themselves as worshiping beings. To what extent do the practices of reformed worship need to be decolonized?

Decolonizing Reformed Worship: Toward Right Relations

Decolonizing perspectives are diverse, but they hold some understandings in common. They affirm the equality and dignity of human persons, and they expose the dynamics of imperialism at play in both cultural practices and everyday actions such as worship. They celebrate the wisdom, creativity, and resistance of those who have been victims of colonial dominance.[44] As Jagessar and Burns write, "The liturgical genres that provide counterparts

41. Aldred, "National Day for Truth and Reconciliation."

42. Aldred, "Canadian Indigenous Realities," Sep 22, 2021.

43. Jones, "Decolonizing Congregational Life."

44. Jagessar and Burns, *Christian Worship*, loc. 369.

for these foci are perhaps bold proclamation, searching lament and generous praise. And perhaps the convergence of postcolonial and liturgical concerns also beckons, or provokes, an invitation to repentance?"[45]

The entire history of Christianity takes place in a colonial ethos. Our worship today continues in cultures that are shaped and influenced by colonialism. "Postcolonialism forces us not only to affirm diversity and resist totalizing tendencies, but also to recognize the partial and limited nature of our findings."[46] To decolonize worship is to recognize that we do not possess the entire story of creation and salvation. Other voices contribute to that story, and we must make room for them in our worship discourses. Decolonizing reformed worship takes into account the ways that spiritual violence may be unintentionally inflicted. It requires examining every aspect of worship in order to identify and transform those aspects of worship, and our identity as worshiping people, that lead away from conciliation/reconciliation instead of toward right relations. The barriers described above should raise our antennae, making us aware of the myriad ways that we try to avoid the work of decolonization. Yet, this work is part and parcel of our call as reformed Christians—to be continually reforming. This means we should not be afraid to critique or challenge our worship practices. It is a stalwart principle of the reformed tradition that we should question and challenge and change in order to align ourselves more fully with what God is doing in the world.

We are not only called to a ministry of reconciliation but also called to embody it in relation to Indigenous peoples. Eve Tuck and Wayne Yang remind us that decolonization is not a metaphor. The term decolonization must refer to Indigenous peoples and their existence on the land. It is not a metaphor for other things, even positive things, such as social justice. When we use decolonization as a metaphor, we recenter whiteness, extend innocence to the settler, and assume that there is a fruitful future for the settler on the land.[47] Thus, decolonization must not be used metaphorically but must be rooted in actual labor that seeks to concretely address the relationships among settlers and Indigenous peoples. It must seek to end colonial practices. I am arguing that worship equips us for action—which includes political involvement in terms of how we vote, how we influence lawmakers, how we fight for the sacred rights of Indigenous peoples. These tasks must take into account Indigenous perspectives and worldviews and the

---

45. Jagessar and Burns, *Christian Worship*, loc. 389.
46. Jagessar and Burns, *Christian Worship*, loc. 325.
47. Tuck and Yang, "Decolonization Is Not a Metaphor," 3.

knowledge and wisdom of Indigenous intellectuals and activists.[48] The following chapters seek to decolonize worship by attending to and arguing for the abolition of the colonial tendencies of Christian worship in the reformed context.

These moves are unsettling and should be unsettling. They interrupt our familiar frameworks of worship, asking how worshiping congregations may be transformed through real engagement with Indigenous sovereignty and struggle. As Jagessar and Burns forthrightly expound, "We are committed to change rather than to silence."[49] They invite those of us who are caught up in colonial systems and systems of white superiority to "stutter toward speech in the conviction that change is necessary and that silence is not an option for us if it colludes with further practice of imperialism. Resort to silence can be an abrogation of integrity and responsibility."[50] So, let us find our voices so that we may speak into the void of pain and destruction, seeking right relations with all our neighbors. Worship is a relational act, in which we are formed and prepared for right relations. The barriers to this kind of worship may seem intimidating, but it is possible to overcome or reduce those barriers by gently but firmly dismantling the structures that maintain separation and discord.

48. Tuck and Yang, "Decolonization Is Not a Metaphor," 3.

49. Jagessar and Burns, *Christian Worship*, loc. 417.

50. Jagessar and Burns, *Christian Worship*, loc. 417.

3

THE GATHERING

WE GATHER FROM THE north and the south, the east and the west to worship the Holy One. We come, bringing our whole selves, including our histories and various identities. In worship, we are gathered into one body. We gather in a particular place, at a particular time—and this place and time is the container that holds our worship. This chapter considers the gathering time in worship as it can prepare us for the work of creating right relations with Indigenous peoples.

Constance Cherry describes worship according to four "load-bearing" walls.[1] Built on a foundation of biblical worship and focus on Jesus Christ, these walls form the structure of the reformed worship service. The first load-bearing wall is the gathering. "The gathering creates a spatial opportunity for worshipers to be gathered in time, place, spirit and unity as they begin the worship journey in community."[2] She notes that it is God who begins the conversation—God is the one who initiates and sustains the gathering of the faithful.[3] The Call to Worship, for example, is an element of liturgy that should acknowledge that God calls us into the experience of worship, a call to which we are invited to respond joyfully and wholeheartedly. The purpose of the gathering is twofold: to unite the community in God's presence and to prepare to hear God's word.[4] The gathering sets the tone for worship and thus will determine whether the worship is rooted in the triune God, or something else. "Worship is therefore a life-changing experience where

1. Cherry, *Worship Architect*, chapter 3.
2. Cherry, *Worship Architect*, chapter 4.
3. Cherry, *Worship Architect*, chapter 4.
4. Cherry, *Worship Architect*, chapter 4.

we are invited to realize and denounce our power and privileges in order to become credible and authentic comrades of the communities at the margins who are engaged in the salvific mission of turning the world upside down."[5]

Of particular importance for right relations with those at the margins are the land acknowledgment, the prayer of confession, and the assurance of pardon. This chapter also addresses worship with children and touches on decolonizing congregational singing.

Acknowledging the Land

In a recent Zoom meeting with individuals from across Canada, I was asked to introduce myself. I began by stating my profession, my family status, and my hobbies. At no point did it occur to me to identify myself by the land on which I live or have lived throughout my life. This points to the reality that I am alienated from the land. I live in a suburb of a very large city, my meat comes in plastic trays, and I rarely wander through the wilderness trails that surround my home. The land tends not to be important for me because my identity and livelihood feel disconnected from my existence on the land. This is true for many in our culture who experience a sense of alienation from the land. For many, however, the land is essential to both individual and communal identity. The question "Where are you from?" can be a loaded question for some, especially immigrants, who are seeking a new home in a new place but may feel intimately connected to the land they have left behind. Indigenous peoples are likely to begin a conversation by sharing about the land they live on and the communities to which they are connected. This is an aspect of Indigenous communal culture that we can both learn about and honor in our worship services.

The location of our worship matters. By this I don't mean the building, although the church building is an essential place for ministry and worship to happen. Rather, I am thinking about the land on which our churches are built and the communities to which they belong. Long before our churches came to be established in bricks and mortar, there were people living and working on the land. Through a series of treaties, Indigenous peoples articulated relationships with the newcomers to the land, intended to govern the relationship among settlers and Indigenous nations. By acknowledging the territory on which we worship, we are honoring those treaties and those relationships. The land acknowledgment belongs at the very beginning of worship.[6]

5. Carvalhaes, *Liturgies from Below*, loc. 164.

6. The acknowledgment may be spoken or projected, printed in the bulletin or on

The land acknowledgment is specific to time and place and is intimately connected to the geographical location of the congregation. At my
seminary in Toronto, Ontario, the land acknowledgment reads:

> We wish to acknowledge the land on which Knox College oper-
> ates. For thousands of years it has been the traditional land of
> the Huron-Wendat, the Seneca, and most recently, the Missis-
> saugas of the Credit River. Today, this meeting place is still the
> home to many Indigenous people from across Turtle Island, and
> we are grateful to have the opportunity to work on this land."[7]

The Presbyterian Church (U.S.A.) offers the following template for acknowledging the land: "As we gather today, we acknowledge that we are on
the traditional lands of Indigenous peoples. (Name the tribes on whose land
you gather.) We remember that we share this land with other parts of God's
good creation: plants, birds, and animals. (Name native plant, bird, and
animal species.) May we be good neighbors."[8] Note that this template also
explicitly includes the natural environment as the location of our worship.

The specific content of land acknowledgments will vary by location, but in each case, they acknowledge the relationship with Indigenous
peoples as well as the relationship Indigenous peoples have with the land
as its first inhabitants. Land acknowledgments should express gratitude for
Indigenous stewardship of the land.

Land acknowledgments can be awkward and uncomfortable for those
of us who are settlers. First, they recognize that the land does not belong to
us. In a capitalist culture, we are accustomed to valuing people by the land
they own. Land acknowledgments invite us to remember that all things,
including our real estate, belong to the Creator. Secondly, land acknowledgments name and remember the treaties that were made among settler
and Indigenous groups. Settlers are likely to be unfamiliar with the history
of these treaties and their meanings. By naming the treaties out loud, we
are reaffirming their value as well as the value of the relationships that the
treaties moderate. Thirdly, land acknowledgments can be uncomfortable
because of the difficulty that English speakers may have in pronouncing
the names of Indigenous groups and treaties. An organization I belong to
always begins their online meetings with an acknowledgment of the traditional territories on which the participants live, work, and worship. For
some reason, I always experience discomfort when it is my turn to explain
on which territory I live—I am afraid that I will get it wrong, or offend

the website. It is most effective when it is spoken out loud.

7. Knox College, "Vision and Values."

8. Presbyterian Church (U.S.A.), "Sense of Place."

someone, or mispronounce the words. We are apt to stumble over words such as "unceded" or "wampum," in addition to the various Indigenous groups to which we refer. Settler fragility can lead to discomfort when acknowledging that the territory on which we reside does not belong to us. Land acknowledgments should inspire us to take action for right relations, not make us feel guilt or shame. They are living celebrations of a real relationship, and a (albeit token) response to the fractured situation in which we find ourselves.

There are dangers inherent in our acknowledging the territory on which we worship. First, we may put too much weight on the acknowledgment, expecting it to bear the burden of everything that is wrong with our relationship with Indigenous peoples. This is only one tiny step—land acknowledgments are one small piece of a greater project of conciliation/ reconciliation and cannot be the sum total of our response. They can seem hollow and performative if they are not accompanied by real action, a critique often levelled by Indigenous persons. Land acknowledgments should not be merely performative; rather, they should lead to reflection and response. If the same acknowledgment is used weekly in worship, it may become rote. This problem can be avoided by changing the content of the acknowledgment periodically and having different voices present it. Secondly, land acknowledgments can obscure the actual history by naming Indigenous people as merely the stewards of the land rather than sovereign nations. Land acknowledgments might also fail to recognize the trauma that occurred when Indigenous peoples were removed from the land—this was a conflicted and painful process. Thirdly, land acknowledgments may portray dispossession as a state in the past rather than an ongoing reality. Fourthly, if you are creating a land acknowledgment with the support and help of an Indigenous person, it is appropriate to pay them for their labor.[9] Our creation of conciliation-affirming resources for worship should not burden Indigenous peoples. This is true for all aspects of the process of conciliation/reconciliation. Finally, land acknowledgments are controversial and may lead to disrespectful conversations as folks come to terms with their full meaning.

The Prayer of Confession

We come to worship as those engaged in a covenant relationship with God. This covenant of grace and mercy allows us to name before God the ways that we have failed to keep covenant.

9. Kaur, "Land Acknowledgements."

It is a privilege and a gift to be allowed to name our sins before a God who has promised forgiveness. We bring our whole selves into the experience of worship, including our sins and our failures. The prayer of confession is a time to make a public acknowledgment of the ways we have fallen short of God's intention for us. The prayer is both individual and communal, confessing both the sins that we personally have committed and the sins that are of a corporate nature. Rice and Huffstutler propose that there is a danger in corporate prayers of confession that we might seem "to put words into people's reluctant mouths, making them confess things they do not feel guilty about."[10] I disagree, perceiving that we confess communally because we are caught up in systems of power and danger that are much larger than the individual. Sometimes, we pray on behalf of the whole church, naming our complicity and participation in sinful enterprises. While the individual may or may not feel guilty, the wrongdoing belongs to the group as a whole. Guilt is not necessary for confession. I perceive the act of confession to be an essential aspect of reformed worship that honors the priesthood of all believers—the privilege to come before God in honesty, with an intention to change our attitudes and behaviors. By confessing our sins, we bring our worst selves into the presence of the Creator who loves us anyway—loves us enough to have sent Jesus Christ into the world to reconcile us to God. Confession sets us free from the past and allows us to imagine a new future. We make a confession together every week because God's mercy and grace lie at the heart of our identity as a covenant people. We are continually falling down and must be lifted up, over and over.

Our confession of sin is also an essential aspect of conciliation/reconciliation with Indigenous peoples. Although our prayers are offered to God and not to other people, our confession is a public acknowledgment of wrongdoing that names sins against God and neighbor. Before conciliation/reconciliation comes truth-telling, and in confession we tell ourselves and God the truth about what we have done to harm others. This is an appropriate time to name before God the ways that settlers have dispossessed, oppressed, and damaged Indigenous populations. It is a place to acknowledge our fragility and other barriers to conciliation. While the individual might be unsure about their own personal role in violence against Indigenous peoples, the collective must take responsibility for the sins of the past and the present. This includes the role of churches in residential schools and other colonial projects, the ways we have cooperated in the subjugation of Indigenous peoples, our sins against the land itself, and other corporate sins such as individualism that undermines community and white/settler supremacy.

10. Rice and Huffstutler, *Reformed Worship*, 120.

I strongly encourage worship leaders to include these prayers of confession every week for wrongs committed against Indigenous communities. To do so is to make a significant statement about the priorities of the congregation regarding conciliation/reconciliation. Sin is all about broken relationship. Repair, then, is also about relationship.

The wrongs that settlers commit against Indigenous peoples are both historical and contemporary. Sometimes, we are confessing wrongs committed by other people in another time and place. And yet, as reformed Christians, we believe that we belong to the communion of saints, which means that we must bear responsibility for the sins of that communion. This is an uncomfortable reality, as many will feel that these sins belong to the past and should not be passed down from our ancestors. In terms of the contemporary situation, some will feel that they do not participate in the ongoing dispossession of Indigenous peoples. The church as a whole, however, continues to sin by staying silent, failing to enact conciliation, and by participating in economic and social structures that are oppressive. These prayers of confession will make us uncomfortable in other ways. They challenge our self-satisfaction, our privilege, and our behavior. In order to make a genuine confession, we must be prepared to repent and change our ways. Change is always difficult, but repenting—to literally walk a new path—is both our calling and a blessed gift.

Prayer is liberating—it also shapes our identity. Through the prayer of confession we come to understand ourselves as ones who matter to God. Even our sins matter to God, who has designed us for life in worship and life together. The kinds of things we confess also shape our identity. If we want to be a community that takes seriously its own agency in the world, then we must name ways in which we fail to enact that agency. If we want to be a community that loves others well, then we must name those times that we fail to love. If we want to be a community that participates in conciliation/reconciliation with Indigenous peoples, then we must offer an honest accounting of our failure to engage others in dialogue and service. We do not do this alone—the God of the Universe urges us toward strong and whole relationship. Confession potentially turns our guilt into action.

> The world as it exists is never the final answer. With God, the world is always open to becoming something else, always looping and circling into new ways of flourishing. Praying with one another teaches us that we are never done. Through prayers God changes us as we change the world, and God becomes more

significant than we first thought. With God we move, we cry, we
survive, we become, we organize, we struggle.[11]

Prayer, according to Jewish theologian and rabbi Abraham Joshua Heschel,
"is meaningless unless it is subversive, unless it seeks to overthrow and to
ruin the pyramids of callousness, hatred, opportunism, falsehoods."[12] According to Cláudio Carvalhaes, worship itself is a subversive activity, which
focuses on God instead of the empires of this world. In confession, we are
proclaiming a subversive gospel, announcing that our allegiance belongs
only to God and not to empire. This gospel claims that forgiveness and
reconciliation are possible, despite the ways that empire seeks to keep us
separate and divided. When we confess our sins, we are contesting the "pre-
vailing order of injustice and inequality," admitting our participation in this
order and seeking freedom from it.[13] In confessing the broken relationship
with Indigenous peoples, we are not only confessing our own wrongdoing
but also addressing a system that is damaged and damaging. The following
prayers of confession may be useful for congregations seeking to integrate
conciliation into this portion of the worship service.

Prayers of Confession

1. Leader: God, how often have we spoken what we thought to be a joke,
only to see the hurt on the other's face? We did not think that our words
would hurt, but they did. How often have we stood by as someone else spoke
hurtful words, and did nothing? How often have we allowed a stereotype or
a bias to get in the way of actually seeing the individual in front of us?

   All: We confess that we do not always see or hear with our hearts. We
confess that we do not always act with your justice.

   Leader: We sometimes feel that we were not there when the children
were taken from their parents and sent away to school. For most, our parents were not there nor were our grandparents.

   All: We confess that sometimes we don't see why we are being held
to account for the actions of people that we did not know and, so long ago.

   Leader: But, we are the bearers of many blessings of our ancestors of
blood or faith. Therefore, we must also bear their burdens and responsibilities. The last Residential School closed in 1996; that was in our time and we
did not know the truth.

11. Carvalhaes, *Liturgies from Below*, loc. 507.

12. Heschel, "On Prayer," 262.

13. Carvalhaes, *Liturgies from Below*, loc. 158.

All: We apologize for the actions of our country and our churches in running Indian Residential Schools. We seek your forgiveness for what has been done to your children. We seek acceptance of our commitment to justice and our desire to walk toward reconciliation.

We ask for your grace to heal all of us.

Amen.[14]

2. Creator God, from you every family in heaven and on earth takes its name. You have rooted and grounded us in your covenant love and empowered us by your Spirit to speak the truth in love and to walk in your way toward justice and wholeness. Mercifully grant that your people, journeying together in partnership, may be strengthened and guided to help one another to grow into the full stature of Christ, who is our light and our life.[15]

We acknowledge and confess the myriad ways we have failed to be in relationship with Indigenous peoples. As a church, we confess our complicity in the residential schools program. We confess that our indifference, shame and guilt cause us to ignore or downplay the very difficult realities faced by Indigenous peoples today. We confess that reconciliation is a word that scares us, because we feel that we have much to lose. Teach us, Holy God, that reconciliation is a gospel word. Liberate us from our guilt so that we may be free to walk in a new way.[16]

The Assurance of Pardon

Immediately following the prayer of confession is the assurance of pardon. These are words of great joy that are proclaimed in the name of Jesus Christ. In Christ's dying and rising to new life, we are also recipients of new life. The old has gone and the new has come. This proclamation of grace is offered solely by God—it does not represent the mere opinion of the worship leader. For those who freely confess their sins, God's grace and forgiveness is offered. When we confess in public worship, an assurance must follow. It is a reminder that we are released from the power of sin and free to walk a new path. "Confession without an assurance is incomplete. We do not want to end with confession and hope for the best. Rather, we end with our acceptance of forgiveness and the promise of grace."[17] The assurance is spoken directly to the people, and Scripture is a profound source of words that

14. Kairos, "On the Path to Reconciliation."

15. Anglican Church in Canada, "National Indigenous Day of Prayer."

16. Travis, "Sermon."

17. Cherry, *Worship Architect*, 133.

promise forgiveness.[18] As a worship leader, I generally invite the congregation to stand in order to receive the words of pardon, as a means to convey the magnitude of the moment.

God reconciles us to Godself in Jesus Christ. The assurance of pardon is pure gift, to be received and enjoyed. It releases us from the guilt and shame of our sin. The assurance does not necessarily lead to conciliation or reconciliation with others, but it is an important first step. If we are indeed free from our sin, then we are also free to forge relationships with others. It is important to contemplate the significance of what the assurance is saying—no matter the depth and breadth of our brokenness and despair, we are forgiven.

The worship leader might struggle to proclaim forgiveness following a prayer of confession that names the truths about our relationships with Indigenous peoples. It seems impossible that such grace is warranted, especially given the degree to which we fail in our public and private relationships. We cannot move forward, however, if we are mired in disgust over our own behavior. While I was planning a worship service for Canada's National Day for Truth and Reconciliation, I found myself stumbling over the assurance of pardon. It seemed trite, following on the heels of a powerful and poignant confession over the treatment of Indigenous peoples—all the ways that the church has participated in the colonization, racism, oppression. How could we offer such a confession and then receive such grace? Upon reflection, I realized that it is only through our liberation in Christ that it is possible to seek to be reconciled to our neighbors. The assurance of pardon is a proclamation that is absolutely necessary for conciliation/reconciliation to occur. Without both the truth-telling of confession and pronouncement of grace, we are stuck in the familiar patterns of life and relationship. When God forgives us, we are liberated and enabled to make new decisions and create new patterns. The pardon should include a commitment to repairing broken relationships that are at the heart of human sinfulness.

The assurance of pardon may be as simple as "in Christ we are forgiven and reconciled to God," or it may be more complex: Friends, the good news is that Jesus Christ walks with us on the path toward reconciliation. In Christ, we are reconciled to God and liberated from that which holds us back. Praise be to the Creator, the Son and the Holy Spirit. Amen.

18. Cherry, *Worship Architect*, 133.

Worship with Children

Worship often includes a time specifically aimed at children and youth. This "children's time" often occurs in the gathering portion of the service, although not always. This time can be used to teach children about the history and contemporary reality of Indigenous peoples.

When I was a child in school, we learned familiar narratives of exploration and discovery. We learned that explorers came to civilize the "Indians" who were willing partners in the settlement of the land. We knew nothing of residential schools, nor the deteriorating social conditions on reserves and in some communities. It is vitally important that Christians socialize our children in a way that is consistent with conciliation/reconciliation. Children need to be educated about the history of residential schools and contemporary struggles for Indigenous sovereignty. Of course, these topics are difficult and may be painful to approach with children. Some of them will have learned about Indigenous issues in school, but others may not be aware of the situation. We must tell them the truth, even when the truth is hard to hear and hard to absorb.

Charlene Bearhead is the former education lead for the National Centre for Truth and Reconciliation. She says, "Our children are going to grow up with this truth, whether we're ready or not. The best thing we can do as parents is find the courage and know that it's not going to be easy and it's not going to be things that we want to hear. But it's things that we need to hear, and we can learn with our children."[19] Some topics may not be appropriate for children in public worship—such as the existence of physical and sexual abuse in residential schools. These topics are extremely sensitive and will require care and attention beyond what can be given in a worship service.

Children learn best by engaging with stories that bring people and situations to life. Children are naturally curious about how the world works, how it is structured, and how we come to live in relationship with one another. The worship movements "Children in Worship" and "Godly Play" offer us an opportunity to engage with children's wonderment.

> Wondering opens the creative process and draws both the lesson and the child's life experience into the personal creation of meaning. The joy that results is far different from the frantic buzz that comes from rewards and punishments or the agitated state that often accompanies trivial entertainment. Joy is a combination of the happiness of finding a way to cope with the limits

19. Schiedel, "Why Our Kids Need to Learn."

to life and the sadness of knowing that there are such ultimate boundaries. Joy is deeply realistic about life and death.[20]

We can encourage children to wonder about others, especially Indigenous peoples. We can encourage them to ask questions, to learn, and to discuss even very difficult topics. We might question the wisdom of teaching children about tragic and terrible stories; yet these stories form an important part of the history and ethos in many nations. If we are to move toward conciliation/reconciliation, then children are part of the process, as they belong to the church as a whole. They too must learn a vocabulary of confession and assurance. They too must learn the painful history and be taught to imagine a future that is different from the past. It is important that parents are allowed to "overhear" the education we are giving their children, so that the family can process the information together. This kind of worship connects us to a broader community than just our churches or our schools. Children are made aware of the presence of others, their relations from other nations and communities. We can also engage them on matters of creation care. Our circle grows wider as we bring these others into the presence of God in worship.

There are plenty of resources that are helpful for talking to children about residential schools and other issues, including children's books by Indigenous authors.[21] These books and stories help us to teach children in age-appropriate ways. Monique Gray Smith provides these concrete tips for creating safer spaces for these conversations to happen:

- Who am I and where am I at? Some people have a hesitancy to talk about residential schools if they are not part of their lived story. It's ok to not know everything. The important thing is knowing now, together.
- Go to Elders for guidance. Not everyone has this privilege, but if you have Elders, ask them what they think needs to happen for a conversation to feel safe.
- Share that children were hurt, but without providing details of abuses. This is developmentally appropriate and as a rule it acknowledges kids are all coming from different experiences and information. "Hurt" to someone who knows about trauma will speak volumes. It's just as strong to someone who doesn't know trauma. The details will be asked later when children are older and ready.

20. Berryman, *Complete Guide to Godly Play*, 45–46.
21. Presbyterian Church in Canada, "Reconciliation Activities for Children."

- Human rights laws. Smith says it's important to let children know there are laws in place now to protect children all over the world. This will let them know there has been forward movement, and they have a right to feel safe.

- Create a space for the conversation. This means turning electronics off. No TV. No phone ringing. No checking social media if it beeps. To respect the conversation is to give it full attention.

- Find out what they know. Kids talk and they will hear things. Ask them what they know and work from there.

- Why don't they know? That question might be an expanded theme for older kids who ask why it's not in schools. It's key to tell kids there were deliberate attempts made to not disclose information about the residential school experience. The fact not everyone learned this in school is a huge part of the discussion.

- Make sure it is a two-way conversation. Pause for their emotions to come out, and your own. It sets a good example for them—you are sad, hurt, overwhelmed. It's human and healthy.

- Sit close. Human contact will reduce cortisol levels that come with stress. Smith notes that is a need we can meet as simply as by holding their hands while we read or speak of residential schools.[22]

The following story was written by children's educator and author Laura Alary for a resource on the United Nations Declaration on the Rights of Indigenous Peoples. It may be helpful to explain to the children that Indigenous people were the first people to live here, before any of us came to live here. Adults should be aware that Attawapiskat is a town located in what is known as Northern Ontario, which has had a suicide crisis, in case they are asked questions about this matter.

Shannen and the Attawapiskat School

Once every year, the people of Attawapiskat go out into the bush for the spring goose hunt. For two weeks they camp together by the river, hunting, fishing, and trapping, just as their ancestors have done for thousands of years.

22. Energeticcity Staff, "Gentle Truth-Telling."

Shannen Koostachin always looked forward to the goose hunt. She loved being outdoors with her mother and father, sisters and brothers, and her many friends, young and old. There was so much to learn: where to find berries, how to track small animals, how to make and tend a fire, how to imitate the call of the geese. There was always plenty of fun and laughter and good food—hot bannock and roast goose and s'mores cooked over the campfire.

At night the elders told stories and legends from long ago. In the circle of the firelight, Shannen snuggled up to her father. She felt warm and cozy.

"It feels good to be here," she said.

"You are part of this place," answered her father. "Part of the water and the land, part of the ancestors who came before you, and part of those who will come after you. We are all connected. Together we keep the circle strong." Shannen felt proud to be part of something so wonderful.

"I wish I felt this good about school," she said.

"Someday you will," her father replied. "Never give up. Just keep walking in your moccasins."

It was hard for Shannen to feel proud of her school. For one thing, it was not even a real building. Shannen and her friends went to class in portables. The portables were small and crowded and not to built to last. There were cracks in the walls and mould around the windows. The doors did not shut properly, so in the winter, icy winds blew in and Shannen's fingers grew so cold and stiff she could hardly write. Mice crept inside to find shelter. Now and then Shannen found them scampering over her sandwich at lunchtime. Simply going to gym class meant a ten minute walk outside, even on the most bitterly cold winter days. Even going to the bathroom was a problem. Because the portables were so tiny, the bathrooms were almost right in the classroom. You could hear everything.

"It's so embarrassing," complained Shannen. "Why can't we have a real school? With proper bathrooms and a gym and a library. Other kids have warm and comfy schools. Why can't we?"

Once there had been a real school in Attawapiskat. Shannen could remember going to kindergarten there. She had paraded through the hallways in her costume at Hallowe'en, and sung carols in the gym at the Christmas assembly. Everyone had been very proud of that school. But one day a pipe burst beneath the building. Diesel fuel poisoned the soil and air. Children were getting sick, so their parents stopped sending them to school. All the students were moved into portables. It was supposed to be for a short time, just until the mess was cleaned up. But seven years later the children were still waiting. The old school building sat empty, surrounded by an ugly chain link fence. Every year it grew more run-down. No one was proud of it now.

Finally, when Shannen was in grade eight, the government of Canada made a plan. There would be a new school—a real school, with hallways, a library, and a gym. Shannen was so excited! Even though she was graduating and would never have a chance to go to the new school, she was happy for her younger sisters and brothers, and all the children who would come after.

But the plan fell apart. The government said no. There was no money for a new school.

"How can they say no?" wailed Shannen. "A promise is a promise!"

"They don't care," said some of her friends. "Those leaders are not like our elders. They live far away. They don't see our problems."

"Then let's help them see," said Shannen.

So they did.

One winter day, all the students—even the youngest ones—stood outside in the icy wind holding signs. *We've never seen a real school*, said one. *If the government has its way we never will.* Photos of the children standing in the cold ended up in newspapers around the country.

Shannen and her friends wrote to the government of Canada to ask for help. But they knew their voices alone would not be enough. They needed to make the circle bigger. But how? They were just a few young people in a small community far from anywhere. But they were determined to get their school. So they called on other students for help. They made videos and posted them on YouTube. They asked other young people to write letters to the government too. Little by little, word spread.

One day Shannen was asked to make a speech at a school in another northern community. This school was beautiful—bright, cheerful, warm. The halls were full of First Nations art, and the sounds of chanting and drumming. Shannen felt good to be there, but sad too. She could see that the students at this school were doing work that was much harder than what she and her friends were doing back home.

"If only we had a school like this," thought Shannen. "Just imagine what we could learn and do and become."

Some days Shannen got tired and discouraged.

"Keep going, Shanshann," urged her father. "Don't give up. Just keep walking in your moccasins. Take your strength from those who came before, and remember those who will come after you. Together we make the circle strong."

Shannen kept going, making speeches, writing letters, telling their story in different places. She travelled all the way to Ottawa, to Parliament Hill, where the leaders of the country meet to make decisions. The man who had said no to building the new school invited Shannen to meet with him. They met in a beautiful room with high wooden ceilings, a marble fireplace, and rows and rows of bookshelves.

"How do you like this room?" he asked. Shannen was quick to answer.

"This room is bigger than our whole portable. I wish my brothers and sisters had a classroom this nice."

But the answer was still no.

Speaking to the crowd outside, Shannen said, "I was always taught by my parents to stand up and speak for what I believe in. I told him the children won't give up. We will keep moving forward, walking proud in our moccasins until we are given justice."

The more Shannen spoke, the more people listened. The more they listened, the more they cared. Students, teachers, churches, school boards—all across Canada and around the world people opened their eyes to the needs of the children of Attawapiskat. The circle was getting bigger and stronger. It seemed like nothing could stop Shannen.

But one day something did. While travelling with a friend, Shannen was killed in a car accident. Her family and friends gathered in a healing circle to share their sadness. They wondered what they should do. Shannen had dreamed of a new school. But more than that, she wanted the children of Attawapiskat to be proud of themselves and where they came from. And she wanted them to be free to imagine where they might go and what they might become. She had always thought beyond herself to those who would come after.

There was only one thing to do.

"We can't give up," they said. "We need to keep walking in our moccasins."

Four years later a new elementary school opened in Attawapiskat. It is bright, cheerful and warm. It has sunny hallways, big classrooms, a library, a music room, bathrooms, and a gymnasium. One of the first big events in the gymnasium was a play put on by the students. The play told legends from long ago, stories of the people who lived along the Attawapiskat River. It told of their connection to the land, to one another, to their ancestors. The play celebrated those who have gone before, those who spoke up for and watched over the community, those who dreamed of a better future. Just like Shannen.[23]

The following questions may assist children in processing this story:
Look back. I wonder who has helped you come to where you are?
Look ahead. I wonder who is coming after you who needs your help?
I wonder how you can make the circle bigger and stronger?[24]

When we include children in the process of reconciliation, we are making the circle bigger and stronger. We will equip them for the work of conciliation/reconciliation, by enabling them to make connections with Indigenous peoples, recognizing their own responsibility and agency.

A Word about Music

Music lies at the heart of worship. Christians have always sung together in worship, both as an act of devotion and as a means of distinguishing themselves from the surrounding culture. As Becca Whitla writes, "Singing has also often been viewed as threatening or even dangerous, especially in Christian contexts. Powerful historical voices have articulated suspicion and distrust of singing (and music) precisely because of its embodied power."[25] The songs we sing together shape our faith and our action in the world. Music inspires us and forms our theology. It is powerful because of its formative nature. As Scottish composer and theologian John Bell writes, "Congregational singing is an identity-shaping activity."[26] Our communities are defined "by the songs that we sing."[27]

What we sing tells us who we are. "Many European ecclesial traditions—their ethos, hymns, bibles, interpretations, liturgies and doctrines—went hand in hand with the colonial enterprise to affirm production, control and domination consciously or unconsciously."[28] It can be problematic when our hymns and songs contain imperial or triumphalistic imagery. Favorite hymns, such as "How Great Thou Art," can be seen to present God

---

23. Alary, "Shannen and the Attawapiskat School."
24. Alary, "Shannen and the Attawapiskat School."
25. Whitla, *Liberation, (De)Coloniality, and Liturgical Practices*, 2.
26. Bell, "'Sing a New Song,'" 20.
27. Bell, "'Sing a New Song,'" 20.
28. Jagessar and Burns, *Christian Worship*, loc. 1183.

as distant and superior, reinforcing the kind of theological hierarchy that undergirded European colonialism, placing God at the top of the hierarchy with white men just a little lower. "Christians become subjects invited into the imperial throne-room of the divine Emperor."[29] By emphasizing human depravity, this hymn illustrates the kind of ideology that led to colonialism—the perception that some people are in need of being civilized. The hymn "Dear Lord and Father of Mankind," aside from its sexist language, has a story behind it that underlines its imperial nature. The hymn writer, John Greenleaf Whittier (1807–1892), was reacting to practice of Vedic priests in Hindu worship. The priests consumed a drink that led them to have a religious experience—a deep sense of the divine. Whittier found this practice repulsive and thus wrote against it in the hymn. These Vedic practices were seen as "foolish ways" and the hymn asks God to "reclothe us in our rightful minds, in deeper reverence praise."[30] This is an example of a hymn that furthers the myth that Western worship is superior to the "uncivilized" worship of other religious groups.

Hymns that portray uninvited border crossings, militaristic imagery, the need for others to be "saved" from their "lack of civilization," and hymns that proclaim the superiority of a particular state or nation are not helpful for the work of conciliation/reconciliation. Such hymns have formed settler churches, which view themselves to be superior and others inferior. Ironically, the very same hymn can be liberating. While "How Great Thou Art" was once used to further an expansionist agenda, it was also translated and interpreted by many nations and cultures that have found it to be an uplifting and liberating song. It can thus be seen as both colonial and resistant to the colonial.

Becca Whitla outlines a liberating praxis for congregational singing that can bring us closer to the image of God found in each one of us.[31] This liberating praxis causes us to struggle against any forces that cause oppression or violence. Whitla argues that most of our congregational singing canon has been dominated by Western European Anglo North Atlantic hymnody. This Western origin has caused our hymns and songs to often be designed and performed to further the goals of empire.

> Consider the obscenity and travesty of the personal and cultural damage done by the colonization of congregational singing. Simply changing a few hymns here and there and adding an exotic instrument is insufficient. What is needed is a deep

---

29. Whitla, *Liberation, (De)Coloniality, and Liturgical Practices*, chapter 5.

30. Jagessar and Burns, *Christian Worship*, loc. 1361.

31. Whitla, *Liberation, (De)Coloniality, and Liturgical Practices*, introduction.

engagement that takes the embodied and enacted theology of singing very seriously. What are we saying with our texts? Or even, what multiple meanings can we discern?[32]

Jagessar and Burns ask us,

> Do the discourse, texts, symbols and imageries (of the hymns) perpetuate bondage and notions of empire? How do they represent Black peoples, ethnic minorities, the Other, gender and sexuality? What do symbols and language communicate vis à vis the agenda of empire/colonialism and the politics of location? When is inculturation and the appropriation of other people's songs and music another form of exploitation or a new kind of colonialism?[33]

If we want to pursue a decolonial agenda in our worship services, we will do well to ponder these questions raised by Whitla and by Burns and Jagessar. Our hymns should be tools for engagement and connection rather than division and separation. There is too much to be said here about using music from other cultures or whether Indigenous songs should be included in settler worship. We must be intentional about not appropriating the songs of other cultures, removing them from their original contexts without attention to their cultural meanings.

Worship leaders can pay attention to the theologies embedded in hymnody and seek to choose hymns and songs that are inclusive, honor a God who is actively working toward reconciliation, and say positive things about other cultures and the nature of humanity itself. Singing toward reconciliation may, of course, include emphasizing hymns that proclaim reconciliation not only with God but also with others. If we are to be a reconciling church, so should our singing uphold the work of conciliation/reconciliation.

---

32. Whitla, *Liberation, (De)Coloniality, and Liturgical Practices*, postscript.

33. Jagessar and Burns, *Christian Worship*, loc. 1156.

4

THE WORD

THE WORD IS CENTRAL to worship in a reformed context. Jesus is the Word of God incarnate, and the Scriptures as revelation from God that inform us about the divine nature. The reading of Scripture and the preaching of the word are key aspects of the worship service, constituting what Cherry calls the "second load-bearing wall."[1] Christian worship is the primary context in which the word is collectively read and proclaimed, and we are invited to hear and interpret the Scriptures as a community. There is so much to say about this topic that I have created two chapters to address the reading and interpretation of Scripture and preaching. This chapter will be more about the interpretation of Scripture than it will be about the public reading of Scripture, although that will be addressed.

Colonialism is everywhere in the Bible. For all of human history, women and men have battled over ownership of the land and its resources. Colonialism was the context in which most of biblical history happened and the context in which it was written and interpreted. From the creation stories in Genesis to the majesty of Revelation, land is a significant theme. We can only understand Jesus, for example, if we perceive that he is a colonized subject, interacting with other colonial subjects and the Roman empire. His life and ministry occurred under the oppression of Rome, and the faith that he taught was preoccupied with Israel's own complex history as a nation which both was colonized and acted as colonizer.

Colonialism provides a frame of reference for many texts because it helps us understand the original context of biblical narratives and thus

1. Cherry, *Worship Architect*, chapter 5.

opens up a window for interpreting them as relevant for the present. By understanding biblical characters as traumatized people struggling to persist and survive in the midst of oppression at the hands of external powers, we can perceive parallels to colonial subjects in the modern era. Biblical texts have often been interpreted from a colonial perspective, meaning that Christians have found justification for colonial projects within the pages of Scripture. A decolonizing interpretation will look for alternative narratives, the absent voices, and the potential for liberation from colonial oppression and trauma.

The biblical text potentially functions as both a colonial weapon and a resource for liberation. The stories in Scripture are stories of colonial oppression and subaltern resistance. They are stories in which some are Indigenous, and others have stolen the land. They are stories that tell of colonizers being saved alongside criminals. Biblical narratives are complicated. They are multiple and diverse. As we listen to the dominant narrative, we should always be asking—is this text liberating, and for whom? Marginalized, enslaved, and colonized groups have often found liberation within the Scriptures of the Old and New Testaments, particularly in the stories of the exodus and the resurrection. This chapter ponders the liberative potential of biblical texts, while acknowledging the ways that texts themselves can be problematic, ambiguous, or even destructive.

The Public Reading of Scripture

The public reading of Scripture is a central act within the worship service. Texts are read out loud as well as interwoven into the liturgy itself; for example, in the Call to Worship, hymns, and prayers. Are there aspects of the public reading of Scripture that need to be decolonized?

One of the great strengths of the reformed theological tradition is the practice of interpreting Scripture in community. This shared interpretation is a vital aspect of worship that can prepare us for conciliation/reconciliation. It forms us in the practices of reading together and understanding together. The next chapter will deal with preaching the word, but here let me say that even though we tend to hear only one person preaching about the Scriptures, it is still a communal task. Through the Holy Spirit, the preacher is invited to be in conversation with others within the congregation and beyond. As Indigenous scholar Ray Aldred notes, a good leader listens to everyone and casts a narrative that reflects everyone in the community so that they feel affirmed.[2] This applies to leadership in general but particularly for

2. Aldred, "Master Class," Nov 17, 2021.

the practice of interpreting Scripture and preaching. There is a vast array of resources that will aid worshipers to enter into conversation with a diverse group of co-interpreters. It is vital that the church's scriptural interpretation arises not from one voice but from many.

It is valuable to pay attention to the "voices" that read the biblical text out loud in the context of a worship service. Including different readers with a variety of voices in the public reading of Scripture is an aspect of decolonizing. This will enable more of the congregation to "see" themselves within the biblical witness. It also ensures that the Scriptures are not always kept in the hands of the powerful. If it is always a white male reading the Scripture, listeners of color or women may feel alienated from the communal reading or fail to see themselves reflected in the text. By including a variety of voices, we open up the communal interpretation of Scripture by claiming that it is a word for everyone.

The reformed tradition places a great deal of emphasis on the sacredness of Scripture. Scripture readings are often followed with the ascription "The word of the Lord." When Scriptures are named as God's word, Scripture is given a great deal of authority. I don't want to dispute that authority, but we should be aware of what it means to ascribe each Scripture reading to the "Lord." What shall we do with Scriptures that portray God as a perpetrator of colonial violence, or those that seem to endorse colonial violence? What will we do with Scriptures that have been used as tools of colonial oppression? What does it mean to say "The word of the Lord" after reading a Scripture that seems to command unwanted intrusion into the territories of others? Are these texts authoritative and in what way? We must make a choice whether we will represent God as a perpetrator or one who works in opposition to the forces of colonialism. So often, these traumatic stories simply describe the way that ancient peoples perceived what God was doing, rather than being factual truths. Difficult Scriptures should perhaps be introduced with a few words in order to put them in context and prepare the reader/listener to understand these texts in their contexts. This is not to detract from the authority of Scripture but rather to understand that we must interpret individual Scriptures within the context of the whole Bible, and the larger notions of God that have been identified and accepted by the church. The authority of Scripture is a challenging topic, and one that must be wrestled with if we are to lead worship that uplifts the possibility of conciliation/reconciliation.

Finally, it is important to consider which texts we choose to read in worship and which portions of those texts are included or excluded. For example, while we might read Ps 137 in worship, we may be tempted to exclude the end of the psalm.

O daughter Babylon, you devastator!
Happy shall they be who pay you back
what you have done to us!
Happy shall they be who take your little ones
and dash them against the rock![3]

This portion of the text is clearly arising from colonial trauma. It speaks of revenge as a natural response to pay back Babylon for its mistreatment of Israel. There are many texts which, read out of context, will confuse or disorient listeners. I suggest that these more difficult texts should not be read in public worship unless they are given context, either in the sermon or surrounding the reading of the text. We simply cannot take these texts at face value without some understanding of the colonial context in which they arose.

That said, it is important that we include a diversity of texts that represent the entire biblical witness. "The downplaying (intentional or not) of the inherent diversity within the collection (as is clearly evident in the four gospel accounts and the pastorals) has colonial overtones."[4] As R. S. Sugirtharajah notes, a characteristic of colonial discourse is to reject diversity in favor of an "unvarying and exclusive truth."[5] The Bible is not a singular book with a singular author. "The Bible does not, and can barely be expected to, communicate one core, or central, message or truth. In fact the reality of the Bible can much better be imagined as layers and complexities to 'truth.'"[6] As Jagessar and Burns write, "The Bible envelops multiple voices, sometimes more or less in harmony with each other, yet at other points sharply divergent, even contradictory."[7] Jagessar and Burns suggest that the Revised Common Lectionary has the advantage of placing diverse texts alongside each other so that they may influence our interpretation and allow for a greater diversity of voices. Here Edward Said's concept of contrapuntal reading, which is derived from musical theory, is helpful. Rather than simply placing diverse texts side by side, this method allows for a reading that honors the differences between them. "In contrapuntal method, it is not just that one voice might stand adjacent to another; rather, contrapuntality suggests that voices do more than stand alongside each other in order. They may interject, interrupt, disrupt, upset, and contest."[8] There is a vivid conversation

3. Ps 137:8–9.

4. Jagessar and Burns, *Christian Worship*, loc. 1490.

5. Sugirtharajah, "First, Second and Third Letters of John," 413.

6. Jagessar and Burns, *Christian Worship*, loc. 1490.

7. Jagessar and Burns, *Christian Worship*, loc. 1490.

8. Jagessar and Burns, *Christian Worship*, loc. 1597.

going on within Scripture itself. Despite the many ways that the lectionary is beneficial, Burns and Jagessar note that "while lectionaries offer a diversity of readings from a multiplicity of biblical voices and theological positions, there is a tendency towards a Christological bias, a bias towards the seasonal cycles of the northern hemisphere and power dynamics that favor a particular group (geographical, ecclesial and gendered)."[9] Worship leaders will need to pay attention to the ways that lectionary texts speak to each other and also what Scriptures and voices are excluded by the lectionary.

Biblical Interpretation with a Decolonizing/Trauma Lens

My children have a 3D book with pictures of animals. If one puts on the special glasses that came with the book, the animals jump out from the page. Biblical interpretation is a similar process. We put on special lenses that enable us to see certain aspects with stunning clarity. In this chapter, I am proposing that we put on bifocal lenses. The first kind of vision we need is decolonial—that is, seeking to recognize and undo the damage of colonialism. The second kind of vision we need is trauma—that is, seeking to recognize and honor the traumatic experience of textual authors, audiences, and interpreters. Together, these trauma and decolonizing lenses will help us to perceive colonialism and its consequences in the text, its audience, and its history of interpretation. It is possible to add other lenses, other types of vision that will highlight different aspects of human experience within the text, including lenses of race, migration, feminism, queer theology, etc. This multifocal perspective brings to the fore those who are most vulnerable and marginalized.

    A decolonized reading pays attention to the original text in its context, the audience of that text, the history of interpretation of the text, and its meanings in the current context. In other words, a decolonized reading "will not only give agency to a multiplicity of voices in terms of these and other issues: it will also highlight that the Bible is a complex and problematic textual repository that embodies the historical, socio-political and cultural complexities not only of its own world, but that of the shapers of what we presently have as an acceptable canon and pattern of proclamation and interpretation."[10]

    We do not leave our own trauma and experiences of colonialism behind when we interpret the text. We read it as settlers, migrants, and as Indigenous persons. We read it as those who have lived always in the West

---

9. Jagessar and Burns, *Christian Worship*, loc. 1703.

10. Jagessar and Burns, *Christian Worship*, loc. 1676.

and those who have lived in other places. All of our experiences and perspectives come into play when we interpret Scripture, and we should be
aware of the way that these might enhance or cloud our vision. Chapter 2
described some of the barriers that may prevent the kind of worship that
can prepare us for conciliation with Indigenous communities. Our lack of
knowledge, Western worldviews, positioning as settlers, our fragility—all
of these may contribute to a reluctance to enter into the deeper work of
decolonizing textual interpretations.

Decolonizing biblical interpretation is a highly complex task, and the
present conversation will hardly do justice to the richness of decolonized
perspectives. I want to offer four simple questions that get at the heart of
decolonizing biblical interpretation. These questions are designed to put
both trauma and decolonization at the forefront, resulting in a deeper and
more meaningful interpretation of Scripture. These questions will help us
to interpret toward the sermon. Each question explores colonial trauma,
which is described as a "complex, continuous, collective, cumulative and
compounding interaction of impacts related to the imposition of colonial
policies and practices which continue to separate Indigenous Peoples from
their land, languages, cultural practices, and one another."[11] Colonial trauma concerns the ways that these policies and practices have caused harm in
multiple ways. These four questions search the text itself for colonial trauma.

1. Is there colonial trauma in the text?

Many, but not all, texts will have colonial trauma associated with them.
It may be hidden in the background experience of the characters. This question asks the interpreter to search biblical situations for evidence of oppression, rule by outsiders, unwanted invasion, etc. This kind of colonial trauma,
of course, forms the context for the exodus, the exile, and the resurrection,
three of the central stories by which we live as Christians.

2. Is there colonial trauma in the experience of the author/audience?

The answer to this question will almost always be yes. This question
delves into the context for which the Scripture was prepared. Was it a response to colonial violence, and what is the nature of that response? Some
biblical authors were more likely associated with the colonizer than the
colonized, and each has a different response to the colonial violence and
what it means for the community. This colonization may be resisted, tolerated, or embraced, depending on the author and the moment in history.

3. What role does God play in the colonial trauma?

This can be a difficult question because we will find that sometimes
God is perceived to be the source or perpetrator of trauma. For example, the

11. Mitchell, "Colonial Trauma."

exile traditions claim that God sent Israel into exile in Babylon as a punishment for its sins. Jesus' violent death on the cross appears to be at the behest
of God, and at no point does God step in to prevent the imperial assault.
While it may have been the plan of God, it is ultimately colonial power that
executes Jesus. Where is God while this is happening? Where is God when
Israel has been deported and Jerusalem destroyed? We have to ask difficult
questions about what God is doing in a text.

There are many texts where God is offering healing or the promise of
healing—prophetic visions of the future when Israel is restored to its former glory, or Jesus healing the leper or the hemorrhaging woman; these
are examples of texts where God is actively healing or promising healing in
the future. Whether we perceive God to be a perpetrator of violence as well
as a healer will depend on our understanding of the divine nature and the
authority of Scripture. I am taking an interpretive stance that biblical texts
were written by traumatized people for traumatized people. It is perhaps
no wonder that in their trauma and in the absence of a better explanation,
biblical folks sometimes blamed God for their trauma and oppression.

If God is powerful, why does it appear that nations are more powerful? If God is sovereign, why do other powers gain strength and behave in
destructive ways toward humanity? While it is unlikely that we can answer
these questions, it is important that we ask them. To ask these questions is
perhaps a form of lament, when we complain and grieve before God, knowing that we can say anything at all and we will be heard. It is within the
biblical tradition of lament to ask God to change the current situation, to
intervene and bring peace. Lament is a liberating action because it names
past and present suffering and appeals to God to change the way things are.
Collective lament leads to collective liberation, as it names before God and
before the community all those ways that the status quo is tied to oppression and subjugation. When we lament together, we are staking a claim on
a better future.

4. Is there hope for healing and for whom?

One of our tasks as preachers is to mine the text for good news. This
question wonders about the possibility for healing in situations of colonialism. Is there a message of liberation or perseverance? Is there a message
of hope that promises healing in the future, and for whom is this healing
intended? Some texts will particularly offer hope for the colonized, others
offer hope for the colonizer, and still others offer hope for both. Another
theme that may be relevant here is the healing of the land itself. In the current context, climate concerns are central for many Christians, and particularly so when it comes to relationships with Indigenous peoples for whom
the relationship to the land is primary. Does the text offer healing for the

creation, for the land itself and the manner in which the land is used and stewarded?

In a decolonized process of biblical interpretation, there will be unanswered and unanswerable questions. How do we position ourselves as settlers reading any text against the backdrop of settler colonialism? There are some texts which are especially useful for unpacking a decolonized reading, especially the conquest narratives that appear throughout the Old Testament. Deuteronomy 20:10–18 is one of the stories that explains how the Israelites came to dwell in the promised land. It is a text of violence and conquest. In order to illustrate how this may be read by settlers, I will pose the above questions to the Deuteronomy text, keeping in mind the context of Indigenous-settler relations.

> When you draw near to a town to fight against it, offer it terms of peace. If it accepts your terms of peace and surrenders to you, then all the people in it shall serve you in forced labor. If it does not submit to you peacefully, but makes war against you, then you shall besiege it; and when the Lord your God gives it into your hand, you shall put all its males to the sword. You may, however, take as your booty the women, the children, livestock, and everything else in the town, all its spoil. You may enjoy the spoil of your enemies, which the Lord your God has given you. Thus you shall treat all the towns that are very far from you, which are not towns of the nations here. But as for the towns of these peoples that the Lord your God is giving you as an inheritance, you must not let anything that breathes remain alive. You shall annihilate them—the Hittites and the Amorites, the Canaanites and the Perizzites, the Hivites and the Jebusites—just as the Lord your God has commanded, so that they may not teach you to do all the abhorrent things that they do for their gods, and you thus sin against the Lord your God.[12]

1. Is there colonial trauma in the text?

Canadian biblical scholar Christine Mitchell posits that there are two prescriptions in this text.

> The first, for towns and territories outside the area claimed by God for the Israelites, calls for the pacification of these peoples by surrender or by conquest. Those who surrender enter into servitude, while those who resist are punished but not exterminated. The second prescription relates to those towns and territories inside the land claimed by God for the Israelites, and it

---

12. Deut 20:10–18.

calls for extermination, regardless of whether these populations resist or not. The reason for both of these prescriptions is made clear at the end: the mere presence of the indigenous inhabitants in the Promised Land is a danger because they may teach the Israelites abhorrent and sinful practices. The indigenous inhabitants of the non–Promised Land do not pose the same risk. What is important to note is that it is only a risk: the indigenous inhabitants of the Promised Land are only theoretically dangerous. Yet their presence cannot be tolerated.[13]

While they do not know it yet, the Canaanites and other groups are threatened with invasion by a people who intend to drive them out of the land by whatever means necessary. These are people living in the land—farming, nurturing and educating their young, with homes and lives. Their existence does not seem to matter in this text except as a problem to be solved. There is an assumption in this text that the Indigenous inhabitants of the land are dangerous and will lead the Israelites astray. This rhetoric perhaps highlights Israel's insecurity about its own identity.

Perhaps less obvious is the reality that Israel will become traumatized by its own participation in the violence of claiming the land. They will become settlers on land that was already inhabited by someone else. Their identity as a nation will be blotted by the unjust taking of the land. In this sense, they will carry with them the trauma that comes from being a colonizer, and much of their theological tradition will be preoccupied with understanding what it means to belong to the land.

2. Is there colonial trauma in the experience of the author/audience?

Israel carries within itself the memory of colonial trauma. As slaves in Egypt, they were oppressed by a great power, and that oppression and subsequent salvation are central to Israel's identity. While it only took one day to get Israel out of Egypt, it will take generations to get Egypt out of Israel.

Decolonized readings will pay attention to the ways that the text responds to "others" in the land. Berge suggests that subversive readings of these texts tend to pay attention to the theme of "othering" in the text, either as a part of the ban (*cherem*) directed against the Indigenous population of the land, or through the divine promise to give the Israelites the land— "with great and good cities that you did not build, and houses full of all good things that you did not fill, and cisterns that you did not dig, and vineyards and olive trees that you did not plant (Deut. 6:10–11)."[14] The authors and audience of Deuteronomy are concerned about the presence of others in the

13. Mitchell, "What to Do with All These Canaanites," 82.

14. Berge, "Empire," 103.

land in light of the promises which God has made. They are trying to come to terms with the existence of other people in the promised land. This could constitute a colonial trauma, insofar as Israel must justify its own presence on the land when it is already occupied. What this text actually describes is the rules of engagement for war against other populations. The Israelites were preparing for war, relying on God's instructions and commandments and promises in order to construct their identity as a conquering people. War is inherently traumatic—for all parties. The instruction in Deut 20 clarifies exactly what the relationship of Israel should be to those who already occupy the land. It is a relationship of conquest, in which women and children are "booty."

3. What role does God play in the colonial trauma?

In this passage, God seems to be the perpetrator of colonial trauma. God is instructing Israel to make peace, yet if this peace is not accomplished by the subjugation of the people already existing on the land, it is to be accomplished by war. The text speaks of "when the Lord your God gives it into your hand"[15]—God is clearly the gifter of the land and does not express compassion for the Indigenous other.

There are at least two subjects of colonial trauma in this text—the Canaanites and other peoples dwelling in the land, and Israel (related to their positioning as colonizers and warmongers). It appears that God is on the side of Israel and expects Israel to move into the land regardless of the presence of others. As Osage scholar Robert Warrior observes, the God we read about in these conquest passages does not have a solid record on liberation—while some are made free, others are conquered. In regard to the whole of the Old Testament, Warrior argues:

> The liberationist picture of Yahweh is not complete. A delivered people is not a free people, nor is it a nation. People who have survived the nightmare of subjugation dream of escape. Once the victims have been delivered, they seek a new dream, a new goal, usually a place of safety away from the oppressors, a place that can be defended against future subjugation. Israel's new dream became the land of Canaan. And Yahweh was still with them: Yahweh promised to go before the people and give them Canaan, with its flowing milk and honey. The land, Yahweh decided, belonged to these former slaves from Egypt and Yahweh planned on giving it to them—using the same power used against the enslaving Egyptians to defeat the indigenous

---

15. Deut 20:13.

inhabitants of Canaan. Yahweh the deliverer became Yahweh
the conqueror.[16]

God's power is at work in this, but it does not seem to be liberating for all
people. Instead, it seems to advocate for the superiority of Israel and the
suppression of all others. We will have to decide how to approach this God.
Do we believe that God wanted Israel to possess the land in spite of the
presence of the Canaanites and others? Was the intention of God really to
drive them out by violent means? Alternatively, this can be read as a text
produced by traumatized people, who were simply looking for ways to survive. Regardless, the author clearly believes that God desired and enabled
the action of driving out the Canaanites.

4. Is there hope for healing and for whom?

It appears that Israel is about to find a new home in a new land, which
will at least partially assuage their colonial trauma associated with being
without a land of their own. This passage does not hold out much hope for
the Canaanites and others. Rather, they are to be the recipients of an attack
that will leave them, at best, as servants and, at worst, slaughtered. Their
lives will be significantly impacted by the incursion of the Israelites, and
there is seemingly nothing they can do.

It is important to consider how these texts have been used in the history of the church and society in order to justify the theft of Indigenous
land and the suppression of Indigenous peoples. Laura E. Donaldson, a
Cherokee scholar, begins her essay "Joshua in America" with a horrific story
of the murders of several Indigenous people in Conestoga, Pennsylvania, in
1763 by the "Paxton Boys," a group of Presbyterians. While I will spare the
reader the details of the brutal massacre, it is worth noting the motivation
for the massacre. Donaldson writes, "A local traveler named Thomas Wright
encountered the Boys on their way home from Conestoga. After Wright
expressed revulsion at the deed, a member of the company asked whether
he believed in the Bible, and whether the Scriptures did not command the
destruction of the 'heathen.'"[17] Donaldson goes on to describe the actions of
the Paxton Boys as motivated by

> the ancient Mediterranean practice of the *charam*, or the ritual
> "devotion to destruction" of one's enemies. In the Hebrew Testa-
> ment, the *charam* appears in such passages as Deuteronomy 7:2
> and 1 Samuel 15:3, and is manifested in Yahweh's command that

---

16. Warrior, "Canaanites, Cowboys and Indians," 262.

17. Donaldson, "Joshua in America," 274.

the Israelites kill every Canaanite "man and woman, child and infant, ox and sheep, camel and donkey" (1 Sm 15:3).[18]

A similar command occurs in Josh 3, in which God promises to drive out the inhabitants of the land in order to gift it to Israel as a means of fulfilling the covenant made with Abraham. The Joshua passage, and other Scriptures, appear to justify the colonization and/or annihilation of entire populations in theological terms. It is easy to imagine how such texts may have been used in North America in order to respond to Indigenous populations with violence. This was certainly the case in the Conestoga murders. There appears to be a strong biblical current that justifies colonization.

Donaldson recognizes the similarities among Canaanites and Indigenous peoples today: "Like the Canaanites, we have experienced military occupation, land expropriation, disproportionate incarceration, arbitrary termination, forced labor, and diasporic removal."[19] Robert Warrior's essay argues that although the exodus narrative has been a central text for exploring liberation, it is not an appropriate model for thinking about liberation for Indigenous peoples. Rather, Native Americans are more likely to identify with the people who were already in the land—the Canaanites who were already living in the promised land. Warrior's call is to center Christian theological reflection and political action on the "Canaanites"—both those in the Bible and those that exist today.[20]

What kind of interpretation will we yield if we are to examine conquest texts from a decolonizing perspective? How might our interpretation lead to a deeper engagement with Indigenous peoples in North America today? Settlers approach these texts *as settlers*—we cannot position ourselves on the side of the Canaanites. What happens when we read these conquest texts as settlers, in the context of seeking conciliation/reconciliation with Indigenous peoples? Christine Mitchell perceives that these kinds of texts are struggling to respond to the presence of Canaanites already existing in the land.

> There are indigenous folks and settler-invader folks, there is land, and from the settlers there is clear anxiety over what to do with all the leftover Indigenous folks. Those leftover folks are the ones who did not have the good manners to either vacate or die. Instead, they remain a constant reminder that the

18. Donaldson, "Joshua in America," 274.

19. Donaldson, "Joshua in America," 276.

20. Warrior, "Canaanites, Cowboys and Indians," 261.

conquest is incomplete and contested. So, what to do with all
these Canaanites?[21]

In many ways, texts found in Deuteronomy, Joshua, and Judges all ponder this question. Mitchell argues that a "plain" reading of the text creates
a circumstance in which colonialism can be justified in the current context: "Such an uncritical allegorization might suggest that because ancient
Israelites were commanded to exterminate the Canaanites, so modern
European-heritage settlers of Canada should feel justified in exterminat-
ing the Indigenous Peoples of this land."[22] If we cannot take these texts
at face value, how might we interpret them today in light of the need for
engagement with Indigenous peoples? Mitchell suggests that we must con-
textualize these texts and acknowledge them as colonial fantasies. That is,
in all likelihood these conquest stories are just that—stories. They represent
the attitudes and theologies of the people more than they represent actual
historical fact. In one of these theological strands, God is perceived to be a
gifter of land. In relation to the book of Joshua, Mitchell reflects:

> As a settler myself, can I believe that God made me a gift of
> this land? Clearly our forebears believed it, and the Doctrine of
> Discovery is a part of that belief. But can I continue to believe
> that today? No, I cannot. And the text of Joshua does not believe
> it either. If the land were truly a gift, it would have been empty of
> indigenous inhabitants, and war would not have been required
> in order to occupy it. The text of Joshua contains a paradox: the
> land is a gift, but it must be taken and guarded with extreme
> vigilance.[23]

As it was, the land was not empty, not then and not now. So how may we
approach these texts in a way that will honor the Canaanites? What happens
if we read these texts through the lens of the UN Declaration on the Rights
of Indigenous Peoples?[24] As discussed in chapter 1, the UNDRIP establishes
that "all doctrines, policies and practices based on or advocating superiority
of peoples or individuals on the basis of national origin or racial, religious,
ethnic or cultural differences are racist, scientifically false, legally invalid,
morally condemnable and socially unjust."[25] It is in this climate that we must

---

21. Mitchell, "What to Do with All These Canaanites," 74.

22. Mitchell, "What to Do with All These Canaanites," 94.

23. Mitchell, "What to Do with All These Canaanites," 86.

24. Mitchell, "What to Do with All These Canaanites," 92.

25. United Nations, United Nations Declaration on the Rights of Indigenous Peoples, 3.

examine and interpret our sacred Scriptures. We must deal with Scriptures that seem to advocate for the superiority of one group of people over others. This problem is not limited to the Old Testament. New Testament texts also sometimes seem to advocate for the superiority of groups of Jews or groups of new Christians. The texts themselves may be problematic, but so is their history of interpretation and the ways they have been proclaimed in the church. For example, Jesus' command to go forth and baptize all nations in Matt 28 has been used to justify conquest and unwanted boundary crossing as well as to confirm the superiority of the Christian faith over the faith of all other nations.

What shall we do with texts that appear to contradict the rights of Indigenous peoples of any land? We should tell the truth about how these texts have been used throughout history in order to suppress Indigenous rights. We should contrast their colonial theological perspectives with more liberating interpretations that contradict the notion of a God for whom conquest is necessary or desirable. As I wrote with regard to the whole context of worship, nothing in our scriptural interpretation should contradict what is stated in UNDRIP, not because UNDRIP is a sacred authoritative text, but because it is a document that lays out what respectful relationships might look like among settlers and Indigenous peoples.

Decolonized interpretations do not deny what is written in the scriptural text but will place it in its proper context. They will also consider the contemporary context and avoid affirming the colonial content of Scriptures. For example, with regard to the Deut 20 text, although it clearly states that conquest is God's plan for Israel, we must challenge that notion. The text is not prescriptive for us; it can instead be interpreted as a cautionary tale that describes what may happen when there is considerable unease, even fear, about the ownership of the land. UNDRIP invites us to scriptural interpretation that honors the Indigenous other without claiming superiority. We must speak against the "genocidal imagination" of a particular biblical text,[26] seeking liberation not only for ourselves as settlers but for Indigenous peoples everywhere. Of course, the most meaningful interpretation may come in conversation with Indigenous Christian interpreters.

Sacred Resistance

Resistance is a particular kind of response to the tragedies and traumas of the world. Ginger Gaines-Cirelli argues that "sacred" resistance is a stance, a way of being in the world, and an ongoing orientation to the world. "As

---

26. See Brett, *Decolonizing God.*

followers of Jesus, sacred resistance is at the heart of our being, not just our doing. . . . Therefore, our inward posture centers on God and resists all that is not God, resists all that is counter to the ways of God revealed through Jesus."[27] Resistance is sacred because it is rooted in God's vision of wholeness for the entire creation. It is not rooted in fear, or self-interest, or benevolence, but in the person of Jesus Christ and the prophetic traditions that find their fulfillment in him.[28] This urge to resistance is a creative urge, not defensive or destructive. "In choosing to risk comfort, status, or safety to be in solidarity with another, you participate in God's way, guided by God's wisdom, empowered by God's grace. If you are participating in God's way, you have a share in the creative work because God is always at work creating and re-creating, mending and making new (cf. Isa 43:19; Rom 6:4; 2 Cor 5:17)!"[29]

There is a deep scriptural rationale for such resistance, but as theologian Douglas John Hall has argued, there is "a serious lack of informed Christian leadership helping people to locate in the Scriptures and theological traditions of their faith a rationale for the ethic of resistance."[30] He argues that Protestants should be very familiar with traditions of resistance, as their very name implies. Protestant churches came into being because they resisted the narratives and theologies of the Church of Rome during the Reformation. Every time we confess our faith, we are resisting any narrative that speaks against God's nature and God's love for creation.

I propose that we can adopt a spirit of sacred resistance as we encounter biblical texts that seem to support colonialism, division, unwanted boundary crossing, and the suffering of particular groups. We can resist the interpretations of these texts that have funded the projects of colonialism through the ages as well as interpretations that ignore their contexts and the contexts of the contemporary reader. We can resist interpretations that misinterpret Jesus in order to justify conquest, domination, or the superiority of a particular group. While it may seem strange for faithful Christian readers to "resist" a biblical text, a stance of resistance is encouraged within the Bible itself.[31] The prophets resisted dominant interpretations that supported the status quo and led to the misery and suffering of God's people. While it is within the prophet's role to be countercultural, can we argue that they were counter-scriptural? They were deeply rooted in the faith traditions of Israel,

27. Gaines-Cirelli, *Sacred Resistance*, loc. 193.

28. Gaines-Cirelli, *Sacred Resistance*, loc. 219.

29. Gaines-Cirelli, *Sacred Resistance*, loc. 225.

30. Hall, *Confessing Church*, 335.

31. See Havea and Cowan, *Scripture and Resistance*.

and yet they are continually challenging Israel's self-understanding and its theologies. Jesus frequently challenged the dominant scriptural interpretations of his contemporaries. For example, from the Sermon on the Mount: "You have heard that it was said, 'You shall love your neighbor and hate your enemy.' But I say to you: Love your enemies and pray for those who persecute you, so that you may be children of your Father in heaven, for he makes his sun rise on the evil and on the good and sends rain on the righteous and on the unrighteous."[32] When Jesus says, "You have heard it said . . ." he is challenging and correcting the abuse of scriptural interpretation. Perhaps Jesus is teaching us to hold Scripture more lightly—to recognize that our interpretations are subject to error and omission. As interpreters of Scripture today, we are invited to resist any reading that seems to contradict the gracious nature of Creator God.

In the context of Indigenous-settler relations, we can pay attention to the ways biblical texts have been used to justify and encourage the theft of the land in North America, as well as residential schools, deprivation of Indigenous communities, and white supremacy. It is a reformed principle that "Scripture interprets Scripture." We interpret Scripture in light of the whole story, which speaks of God's great love for all of creation, and God's continual attempts to renew all of creation. Scripture, as a whole, is liberating. The arc of God's care for creation bends toward justice and peace, not conquest or colonization. In Jesus Christ, God has reconciled Godself toward humanity, urging us toward love. Scripture must be read and interpreted within the context of that unfailing, generous love. We read it not in the grasp of death but in the grasp of grace.

32. Matt 5:43–45.

5

THE SERMON

THE SERMON FOLLOWS THE public reading of Scripture within the worship service, forming the second part of the service of the word. Sermons are ongoing conversations among the people of God, the preacher, the Scripture, the culture, and the divine Spirit. In these conversations, we interpret the world and word together, seeking wisdom and guidance for living out our days. Preaching is a formative practice; it tells us who we are and to whom we belong. It tells us that the status quo is not the only possibility. "Christian preachers dare to dance on the grave of despair and sing in the domains of death in the name of Jesus Christ, crucified God-with-us and firstborn of God's new creation."[1]

Preaching involves not only understanding the text and the process of sermonizing but also understanding the human beings involved in the process.[2] As discussed in chapter 2, there are barriers that stand in the way of worship that equips us for positive relationships with Indigenous communities, and these barriers come to bear on the practice of preaching. Listeners may be fragile about race or their positioning as a settler. The traumas of the texts and our lives interrupt our ability to hope and imagine. Often, we prepare sermons without reference to the perspectives of others that may fruitfully inform our preaching.

The sermon is a local event, but it is connected to the larger church and the world beyond the church. The sermon connects us to other Christians in all times and places. In preaching, we join our voices in a much larger

1. Brown and Powery, *Ways of the Word*, loc. 68.
2. Kim, *Preaching to People in Pain*, loc. 186.

conversation about the interpretation of Scripture. I argue that preaching also connects us to other people, even those who are not Christian. In public worship, our sermons address a much larger audience. This audience may not ever hear our preaching, and yet we find ourselves interconnected because all people are interconnected. We represent others in our preaching, speaking about social issues and community issues as well as the needs of "the world." The church must never allow itself to be isolated from this multitude of others. Thus, our preaching addresses the individuals in the pews but must be both sensitive to and aware of the presence of others. They are our relations. For example, Catherine and Justo González remind us that "in a Thanksgiving service, we must be ready to repeat in the presence of our Native American sisters and brothers whatever is said about ownership of the land."[3]

Preaching, then, can equip us with a particular perspective about those who live on the land with us, especially Indigenous peoples. Sermons may focus on issues of conciliation/reconciliation with Indigenous peoples as their main theme or may draw illustrations from historical or contemporary situations. While preachers will probably not preach about Indigenous realities every week, these sermons may be particularly appropriate at certain times during the church and secular calendars. In Canada, for example, we have a National Day for Truth and Reconciliation. This chapter asks, How might our preaching equip us for the work of conciliation/reconciliation?

An Approach to Decolonized and Trauma-Informed Preaching

We preach to mixed company. Within all of us is the potential to be perpetrator or victim/survivor; in fact sometimes we occupy both roles simultaneously. In worship, there will be those who have been abused sitting beside their abuser. There will be those who have committed crimes, those who have told big and little lies, those who have been violent toward others. The gospel is for all of them. All have sinned and fall short of the glory of God. Surely, however, we have a responsibility to protect and prioritize victims/survivors? Like the preferential option for the poor offered by liberation theologies, decolonial theologies will ask us to lift up the experience of the colonized as a priority when we are interpreting texts and contexts.

This segregating of the categories of victim/survivor and perpetrator may not work because perpetrators tend to also be victims. They are victims

---

3. González and González, "Larger Context," 31. They are here referring to celebrations of the American Thanksgiving holiday.

of violence and abuse, victims of systems in which they are pawns, victims of family members, victims of the church. To quote Desmond Tutu:

> Even supporters of apartheid were victims of the vicious system which they implemented and which they supported so enthusi-astically. This is not an example for the morally earnest of ethical indifferentism. No, it flows from our fundamental concept of ubuntu. Our humanity was intertwined. The humanity of the perpetrator of apartheid's atrocities was caught up and bound up in that of his victim whether he liked it or not. In the process of dehumanizing another, in inflicting untold harm and suffer-ing, inexorably the perpetrator was being dehumanized as well.[4]

Human beings fail one another in so many ways. The division between victim/survivor and perpetrator is blurred, and yet the experience of each must be considered. The bottom line is that we preach to both perpetra-tor and victim/survivor, sometimes within the same person. For example, I come to worship as a perpetrator of colonial violence insofar as I am a member of a society that oppresses Indigenous peoples. I am a landowner, a taxpayer, and too often silent in the face of injustice. At the same time, I am a victim of systems that were created before I was born. These blurred identities create pain and discomfort. The pain perpetrators will carry is different than what victims/survivors carry and should not be compared. Each must be approached with respect and sensitivity, recognizing that each carries trauma in their own way, and the worship service should make space for this trauma.

How might we approach the sacred space of preaching when it is filled with both sin and suffering? There is no formula. What I'm offering is a series of approaches to preaching that is aware and sensitive to colonialism and the trauma it causes. These are not steps to be taken but rather ways to approach sermons that take colonialism seriously. These approaches are particularly helpful in situations where the harm has been caused by the church. In order to illustrate these approaches, I relate them to the topic of residential schools.

In Canada, residential schools were established by the Canadian gov-ernment and churches and run by mutual arrangement.[5] With the recent discovery of grave sites at many residential school sites across the country, the issue is on the minds of many Canadians who gather for worship in

---

4. Tutu, *No Future without Forgiveness*, 103.

5. Formal church involvement ended in 1969, when the schools were transferred to the responsibility of the federal government. Many church staff remained in their positions at the schools following this transfer.

Christian churches. Preachers should be prepared for a variety of fragile and traumatic responses when we preach about the topic of residential schools because it is a traumatic subject, inherently. The focus, of course, must be on the trauma of the children, their families, their communities. That trauma is multi-generational and profound and must be honored.

There is other trauma here. The abuse and deaths of children are deeply painful and triggering for many reasons. Settlers may feel guilt or shame or anger arising from the traumatic wounding of being the colonizer. We as preachers may hesitate to approach this topic at all because it is so difficult for so many people, including ourselves. Preachers will have to deal with their own trauma responses in relation to this topic. The following points describe a way of planning and preaching a sermon that takes seriously the complexities associated with preaching about residential schools.

Be silent. In the face of trauma, before we do anything else, we need to listen to the narratives that are being told about oppression and trauma. This will involve sitting with victim/survivors and hearing their stories without inserting our own voices. Before we speak, we must listen.

In preaching about residential schools, it is important to listen to the Elders and Knowledge Keepers within Indigenous communities. It is vital that we stand before the graves of the children and be quiet because we have much to learn. Preachers will benefit from reading books written by Indigenous authors as well as encountering Indigenous art and culture. Of course, we listen for the Holy Spirit, for it is only through that Spirit that there is any possibility we will find words to speak in the face of such tragedy.

Know your audience. As much as it is possible, preachers are invited to learn about the people with whom they preach. There will be secrets, things that you as preacher are not privy to, but you will know enough. You will know that among your listeners are those who have been harmed by the church. This kind of trauma, whether inspired by various forms of abuse, residential schools, or rejection or discrimination against LGBTQI communities will be compounded simply by the experience of entering a church and engaging with church leadership. Others will experience the church as a safer space where they can bring their pain. One of the goals is to make the worship space as safe as possible. It can never be entirely safe—it is, after all, a space of transformation, which is a painful experience. It hurts to be changed. By knowing our audience we will be better able to respond to the needs that are present in the sanctuary.

As mentioned above, our audience is not limited to those who gather for worship. In a digital age, our audience is much larger. There is also an "imaginary audience" to whom we are accountable as preachers but whom we will likely never meet. What we say in worship should be repeatable to these "others." This is a particular ethical stance—to strive to preach words that are faithful and true to the experience of others. This will sound like a heavy order for preachers—to know and understand both those with whom they are familiar and those who are strangers. If we listen well enough, we will be able to hear a variety of voices that can inform our preaching.

When it comes to preaching about residential schools, it is important to know and understand the demographic you are addressing. To whom are you preaching? What is your wider audience reached by social media or by email? What is your imagined audience? What colonialism-related trauma are they carrying? How are they likely to react to preaching that addresses the history of residential schools, especially the church's role in that history? What trauma might be unearthed, or addressed, or healed through your message? For many of us, our audience will not directly include Indigenous peoples. We are more likely to address a mixed group of settlers with varying experiences related to colonialism. As noted above, this group will include those who feel guilt and shame about residential schools as well as those who may feel angry or defensive. Some will want to take personal responsibility, others will believe that the responsibility does not belong to them but belongs in the past. One pastor explained to me that he had both former staff of residential schools and former students in the same congregation. His preaching had to address both groups. We can imagine this to be a challenging task, and one that must be approached with grace and a solid sense of God's justice.

Know your context and understand it in relation to your listeners. This goes beyond watching the news to a deeper and more meaningful awareness and understanding of what is going on in the world. If we are to address colonialism and trauma in our sermons we must know the ways these are affecting our listeners. While we may not have the time or the energy to delve deeply into history and current affairs, we should at least have some understanding of the key issues insofar as they are likely to be affecting the listeners. The invasion of Ukraine in the winter of 2022, for example, was a traumatizing event for many who have fled war-torn countries, been under attack, or lived under occupation.

In other words, preachers need to be aware of the sources of potential harm that exist in our environments. What is going on at a societal level and a more local level that will potentially trigger or discomfit those who are experiencing trauma related to colonialism? These are, of course, the very topics and situations that must be addressed in preaching in order to respond to what is going on in the minds and hearts of our listeners. If there are traumatizing events happening in the world, then we should have something to say about them in the pulpit.

As more graves are uncovered, it will be important to pay attention to how these terrible events affect Indigenous peoples and settlers. These events may be on their minds as they listen to us preach whether or not we are actually speaking about them in a particular sermon. In order to be equipped to preach on this topic, it is wise to educate ourselves as much as possible about the history of residential schools. What harm has been done and is continuing to be done?

Honor the multiplicity of human psychology and experience. Human beings are complex. It is possible, even typical, to be vessels of both sin and grace at the same time. We can be good people and still participate in racist or colonial practices. Indigenous peoples are diverse and cannot be described or represented without careful consideration of stereotypes and discriminatory perceptions. Trauma will be experienced differently by different populations—all are valid but unique and should not be compared or equated.

When it comes to residential schools, the children are the victims, as are the families and communities from which they were stolen. They were victims of women and men who likely (and erroneously) thought they were doing something good. These staff of residential schools were also victims of a system that placed human life in a hierarchy with white superiority at the top. In some manner they were playing their part in a system from which it was difficult to be extracted. We understand that today as we are confronted with the reality of residential schools—we recognize the ways that we are caught in systems of injustice that oppress and maim. It would be rather challenging, for example, to try to live outside of the capitalist system. So, it is challenging for us to live outside of a colonial system, and we are also victims of it. Settlers today are left with a legacy that we don't want to carry, a situation that we did not cause, and which we perpetuate even without our full knowledge and consent. The sins of the past have come to haunt us in the present. Perhaps we are all victims of the past, although I want to repeat that it is Indigenous communities that carry the weight of that past sin. Settlers today carry the burden of the sins of the church but will need to unravel the threads of colonial power that remain present in their attitudes and behavior today.

Interpret Scripture using a decolonizing lens coupled with a trauma lens. The questions I provided in the previous chapter are helpful for shaping a sermon:

Is there colonial trauma in the text?

Is there colonial trauma in the experience of the author/audience?

What role does God play in the colonial trauma?

Is there hope for healing and for whom?

When asked sequentially, these questions function as a model for a sermon that goes from suffering to hope. Such a sermon will keep colonial trauma at the center and search the text and context for the existence of colonial trauma. These sermons will need to address the manner in which people's experience of God has led them to thwart or embrace colonial ideologies. As noted previously, this is a difficult step, because we may have to come to terms with a God who seems to encourage colonial activities. Many texts will offer redemption or hope, and these themes constitute good news.

Telling the story/naming the harm. Desmond Tutu writes, "It is not the trauma itself that defines us. It is the meaning we make of our experiences that defines both who we are and who we ultimately become."[6] Meaning-making is a task of the sermon as we attempt to weave past and present trauma and future hope into a present that makes sense. When we tell stories, we are attempting to take bits and pieces of our experiences and weave them into a narrative. We know that with trauma, narratives sometimes resist being told, as trauma inhibits capacity for language and meaning making. It is vitally important that we tell the stories of trauma—of those who were lost, those who survived, and those who continue to exist in a traumatized space. Storytelling is essential: "Telling the story is how we get our dignity back after we have been harmed. It is how we begin to take back what was taken from us, and how we begin to understand and make meaning out of our hurting."[7] Tutu goes on: "How we begin is by first letting the truth be heard in all its rawness, in all its ugliness, and in all its messiness."[8] In more poetic terms:

> To whom shall I tell my story?
> Who will hear my truth
> Who can open the space that my words want to fill
> Who will hold open the space for the words
> that tumble out in fast cutting shards
> And the words that stumble hesitantly into the world unsure of
> their welcome.[9]

In our sermons we can open up a space to tell the story and name the harm. This will not be an easy task because we must first listen and then be able to find words that can knit together the experiences of someone else. It is better if we can tell people's stories in their own words or, better yet, invite them into the pulpit to tell their own stories. If we are to do this, we need

6. Tutu et al., *Book of Forgiving*, 70.

7. Tutu et al., *Book of Forgiving*, 71.

8. Tutu et al., *Book of Forgiving*, 74.

9. Tutu et al., *Book of Forgiving*, 88.

to be aware that telling one's story can be retraumatizing. Individuals must be comfortable enough to speak, and they must receive support that will enable them to perform this difficult task. Preaching has always implied that one person is delivering a sermon to a gathered community. A decolonizing perspective on preaching will question this binary and hierarchical division of pulpit and pew. It may be possible to include dialogical or conversation elements in a sermon that allow a multitude of voices to participate in the truth-telling.

In the sermon, we have an opportunity to tell the stories of residential schools and to recount the harm. This is an important step in the healing of trauma, for narratives to be spoken aloud and for the harm to be named. The harm of residential schools is very clear, but it is important that we explicitly identify the historical and ongoing implications of colonialism in relation to residential schools. The harm is immeasurable, but even naming that is an important step.

Try not to reproduce harm in the sermon. Some sermons will lead to trauma responses. We cannot prevent that from happening. In fact, sometimes those responses are helpful and adaptive or lead to transformative change. It is important, however, to reduce harm as much as possible and certainly to avoid reproducing the harm within the sermon. We may reproduce harm in the sermon if we use lenses that are colonial, sexist, racist, exclusive, etc. We might reproduce the harm in a sermon, for example, if we were to use colonial interpretations of a text in order to preach to an Indigenous congregation. Similarly, we might reproduce harm if we failed to portray the diversity of Indigenous communities or offered thin or inaccurate representations. Harm would be reproduced if we were to interpret the text in such a way that blamed the victim for their own trauma. The harm can be much more subtle—the privileging or excluding of particular voices or the exclusion of particular groups from sermon illustrations or examples. We reduce harm when we are cautious and careful with our words and when we hold ourselves accountable by following a decolonized interpretive perspective and/or a method for trauma-informed preaching. Obviously, we must be careful with how we represent the pain and trauma of others in a sermon. When it comes to residential schools, the story is an extraordinarily painful one for everyone who hears it. It will take both decolonial and trauma lenses to begin to unpack the implications of residential schools for church and society.

Accountability and confession. The church must hold itself accountable for harm it has done. Sermons are a place to confess the sins that have caused trauma—including all forms of abuse, colonization, and exclusion. It can be powerful for those who are experiencing trauma to hear such a confession. This is about naming the harm that the church has caused by its participation in residential schools. This aspect will be particularly painful for settlers. It is traumatic to consider that the church causes harm at all, let alone to accept that the church willingly joined and encouraged the government in its administration of residential schools.

"Forgiveness is a conversation."[10] I am so grateful to Desmond Tutu for this quote—because forgiveness is not easy or straightforward. Forgiveness is a long and complicated conversation, a form of negotiation, in which we name harm and seek healing from God in hopes that the divine healing will aid our human relationships. The concept of forgiveness lies at the heart of our preaching, as it is one of the gifts that God has given and is meant to be proclaimed. Forgiveness, however, is not always possible when people have harmed one another. It can feel like a burden we are unable to bear alone.

When it comes to our struggles with forgiving others, Joni Sancken suggests that God holds forgiveness like a gift: "We can trust God to hold forgiveness as a gift and promise rather than a burden to be thrust on those who have suffered injustices."[11] Forgiveness has often been used as a weapon, a means of wielding power so that victims feel that they must forgive if they are to be faithful to a God who seems to demand forgiveness. God forgives us long before we forgive each other. The miracle, of course, is that God not only heals our sins, God also heals the sins of the perpetrator. While we as preachers proclaim forgiveness from God, that forgiveness comes with a responsibility for truth-telling and repair. We cannot offer forgiveness on behalf of another—the victim must have agency to forgive on their own terms. We can encourage individuals to forgive themselves, as self-blame, guilt, and shame are such a burden for survivors of colonial trauma.

Forgiveness is complicated, but what is not in question is the quantity and quality of God's reconciling love for us. In Christ, we are forgiven, we are a new creation. And yet in a variety of ways we continue to participate in systems that oppress and kill. Residential schools are no longer operating, but they are a recent and deep wound that will repeat for generations. I don't like the idea that we should proclaim forgiveness for the architects and workers of residential schools or for the church for supporting the project. I suspect, however, that the miracle is that just as God has forgiven our sins, God forgives theirs. There is a different process when it comes to forgiveness within the human community. Is it appropriate to ask Indigenous peoples for forgiveness for the murder of children and the harm done to entire

10. Tutu et al., *Book of Forgiving*, 7.
11. Sancken, *Words That Heal*, loc. 1466.

cultures? Forgiveness seems unlikely until we have listened to accounts of the harm that has been done, engaged in continued conversation, and offered reparation. I will further address the topic of forgiveness in chapter 6, in the context of communion.

Accept that we can't make it all better. Despite our best efforts to raise awareness and address issues of colonialism, the trauma remains. Occasionally we make it worse by attending to subjects that cause discomfort and pain. There is literally nothing we can say that will erase the trauma of residential schools. It is truth, and this truth must not be covered up or buried. So, we can tell the truth about what happened to those children and their families. While we always hope that our preaching will transform someone or something, we must not be over-enthusiastic about the potential for transformation within a sermon about residential schools. It is horrible news, and the good news of the gospel does not make it any less horrible. There is good news—God is at work in our preaching and may be able to accomplish what we cannot. We cannot make it all better. It is unlikely that these sermons will end with anything other than a cold and broken hallelujah.

Handle gospel with care. Elsewhere I have written about having a conversation with a traumatized friend and my desperate urge to get to resurrection.[12] I wanted her to get over it, get past the difficult part, and get to the good, easy part. She was not ready to do that. She was not ready to see the whole brightness of the message. She needed to sit with the grief and the trauma as it gradually healed, like the sun rising, not like a sudden flash of light. Healing happens more slowly in real life, in general, than it does in biblical texts. When we preach resurrection, it may be a slower and more gentle coming to life, which may be more imaginable for trauma survivors. Be aware of the brightness of the message. The feeling of coming out of the dark into the bright sunlight is familiar. It makes our eyes squint and causes us to sneeze. It's too much, too soon. Preaching can be like that. We like to dazzle with good news, but it might be a bit too much for those bearing traumatic wounds. Perhaps we should seek pinpricks of light that won't hurt anyone's eyes.

I have been taught that the purpose of preaching is always to proclaim the good news of Jesus Christ. I still believe that is true but in a much more nuanced way. Preaching is always good news, for everyone, in the cosmic sense—that the triune God has loved us so much that Jesus came to show us how to live, and to die, and to rise up again. That is good news and should

---

12. Travis and Wilson, *Unspeakable*, 32.

be proclaimed in every sermon. The good news of God's reconciling love in Jesus Christ will be comforting for both victims and perpetrators.

The message of the gospel is often a difficult one for perpetrators. It will likely sound like bad news before it sounds like good news. The gospel call to confess and repent does not sound like particularly good news. In actuality it is awesome news, the best news. However, the call to confess and repent may be troubling to those who stand to lose something—for the rich or the powerful, or for the abuser or the colonizer or the racist who has caused trauma. The good news offered to victims/survivors sometimes involves a change of status for the rich and powerful—or the oppressor or the abuser. That is, the powerful stand to lose what the oppressed stand to gain. This is, of course, gospel news—that there could be a more equitable distribution of wealth and power. It certainly doesn't sound like good news to the powerful one who is about to lose their power! The victim may also be hurt or challenged by the fact that good news is offered to their abuser. It may feel like their abusers are being rewarded or exonerated. It is impossible to sort out all the nuances of gospel here. My point is that while victim/survivors and perpetrators may experience good news in different ways, there is healing and transformation available for both. Care is needed to consider how each group might hear and interpret good news.

It's hard to find good news when we are preaching about residential schools. It is not good news that children are dead, and it was covered up, and nothing is being done to bring justice. It is not good news that the church that was entrusted with the sacred task of caring for children allowed them to be separated from their families and abused and killed. There is grace somewhere in this mess. There is grace operating at a wider level as the Holy Spirit cries out when we cannot find words. The good news of Jesus Christ is that God came to reconcile Godself to us. There is also the good news that we have this ministry of reconciliation.

Reconciliation is a gospel word. It is good news, but what does it actually mean in the context of residential schools? God is the source of reconciliation, and God is reconciling us to Godself in Jesus Christ. The threads of relationships among settlers and Indigenous peoples, however, are so tenuous as to be almost nonexistent. Therefore, it is more accurate to talk about conciliation than reconciliation, at least when we are talking about human relationships as opposed to our relationship with the divine. Conciliation may not sound like good news, because to enter into relationship with Indigenous peoples, which is required by any process related to reconciliation, settlers will have to give up something, at least in terms of power. Thus, settlers may first hear the good news as bad news. It will not sound like good news that conciliation requires truth-telling and confession, accountability and restitution. Those are preciously difficult offerings to be brought by settlers in the worship space. The work of conciliation is hard, and messy, and will not happen without generous self-giving and deep introspection. Self-giving never sounds like good news. It is, of course, wonderful news—that we are invited to pour ourselves out for the world, just as extravagantly as God pours divine spirit into us.

Preach hope, anyway. I have frequently had the experience of approaching a text that proclaims restoration or wholeness and wonder whether I have the capacity to preach anything at all when the current situation is so dismal and hope seems so elusive. It is sometimes an excruciating experience to preach in the midst of colonialism and trauma. The prophets are excellent role models for what it means to be called to speak good news and bad news to the people. It is our vocation to speak the good news of Jesus Christ no matter what. Even when the sky is falling, we have to find words of comfort and challenge. We preach hope even in the worst situations because we believe that God has given us a hope beyond the present that informs and shapes the present. We preach hope even when we don't have any words to express it, and we have to rely on the words of others. Sometimes we may even have to borrow hope from others.

It will take both a prophetic and pastoral imagination to see hope when it comes to residential schools. The past cannot be undone, although there is a certain grace in naming the harm out loud. The hope lies in healing the brokenness. While there is no such thing as an easy conciliation, there is hope in the reality that there is room for growth and development. There is hope in the notion that settlers might divest themselves of power and land in order to make restitution to Indigenous nations. There is hope in the ways that survivors have managed not only to survive but to thrive even in the worst circumstances and amid so much trauma. There is hope that we might listen to the voices calling us from the grave to be gentle with children, especially those who are caught up in systems of violence and oppression. The gospel hope is that all of us can be made free from the systems that bind us—whether we are perpetrators or victims/survivors or something in between. In the case of colonization, there is hope that we can resist neocolonialism and imperialism so that we are ready to come to the table with Indigenous peoples in a spirit of mutual respect.

Some would argue that Jesus Christ has already freed us from these systems. Certainly, the message of the resurrection is that the powers of death are illusory. The injustices continue, however, so we will rightly wonder where God is in all of this tragedy and trauma. The promise and the hope of gospel is that God is right here in the midst of it all. Some will not be able to feel any hope at all. In those situations, perhaps we as preachers hope on their behalf. There is an invitation here to see beyond what seems possible. The hope of healing, the hope of conciliation/reconciliation, rests not in our hands but in the triune God. Even if we can't see it, the hope is always there. The moon is always there, always whole and round, but we can't always see the whole. We see it partially. Hope is like that. It is always there, whole and perfect, but we can't always perceive it in its entirety. God holds hope like a gift, and we are able to perceive it as we are ready.

The following is a brief sermon prepared for the 2021 National Day of Truth and Reconciliation in Canada. It is intended for a congregation of settlers and focused on 2 Corinthians 5. The sermon roots the task of reconciliation in our baptism.[13] It is a sermon that tells the truth about the gospel and its implications, protests the status quo, and seeks to prepare settler Christians for the ongoing work of conciliation/reconciliation.

On this day, we are invited to reflect on the task of reconciliation. We remember the children who never came home—those who were forcibly removed from their families and whose voices now whisper to us from the grave. We remember those who have survived. We remember the harsh conditions still experienced by Indigenous communities. We remember the Calls to Action of the Truth and Reconciliation Commission. We remember, and we hope that we will find a path toward reconciliation.

Reconciliation is a gospel word, yet it can seem like bad news for those of us who consider ourselves settlers on the land, those of us who are not Indigenous, but bear the responsibility to work toward right relations. Reconciliation first sounds like bad news, because it will take tremendous effort and a decentering of self in relation to others. It makes us so uncomfortable.

It will cost us something.

There are over one hundred Indigenous communities in this land we call Canada that are under boil-water advisories. Imagine if the water flowing from your taps in your home was not safe to drink. This is the situation for many. Two weeks ago, the community of Shoal Lake, for the first time since 1997, has clean water flowing through its taps. I read that some residents were suspicious—they found it hard to believe that they could trust the new water treatment plant that has been installed. What does water have to do with reconciliation? It is a human right to have access to potable water. Projects that reverse boil-water advisories are essential to the infrastructure of reconciliation.

Water is part of the earth. It is a gift from the Creator—meant to be enjoyed and shared. It is part of our connection to the earth and thus to the

---

13. Travis, "Sermon."

Creator. There is another way that water matters when it comes to reconciliation. As Dr. Ray Aldred of the Vancouver School of Theology puts it, baptism is our creation story.[14] Baptism tells us who we are and how we are related to others. The waters of baptism are essential for right relations in the here and now.

As the apostle Paul writes in 2 Corinthians 5, anyone who is in Christ is a new creation. The old has passed, and the new has come. These words are a reminder that in baptism, we die and rise with Christ—our sin is drowned with us, and we are reconciled to God. I have to tell you that I hesitated to include an assurance of pardon in this service. It seems like such an audacious claim—that we can be forgiven and made new even in the midst of the terrible history and the continuing consequences of colonialism. We must not confuse this pardon with forgiveness from Indigenous people—which may or may not come. Rather, we are reconciled to God in Jesus Christ. Our repentance, as baptized people, is ongoing. We must confess over and over, and be forgiven by God over and over. Repentance precedes baptism, and it continues, because we are prone to failure. This is good news. This is the best news, because in being reconciled to God there exists the possibility that we can be reconciled to one another. We have this ministry of reconciliation, in which we are called in partnership with God, to heal the divides and crevices of our relationships.

It has been made very clear to me by Indigenous folks that the burden of responsibility for reconciliation with Indigenous communities lies with non-Indigenous people. Settlers are responsible for confessing historical and contemporary truths. Settlers are responsible for teaching our children to do better. Settlers are responsible for making things right, so that a renewed relationship can unfold.

We are responsible, but we are not alone. We have been prepared for such a time as this by the waters of baptism. These waters literally recreate us, into followers of Jesus' way. These waters set us free from the power of sin and cleanse us from unrighteousness. These waters equip us for the work of reconciliation with Indigenous peoples and all others from whom we are estranged.

These waters help to ease our discomfort so that we can listen intently to the voices that call for justice.

Reconciliation is an impossible task if it is not rooted and grounded in the Creator as the Creator is made known to us in Jesus Christ. On this day, as we reflect on the task before us, may the waters of baptism flow over us,

14. Aldred, "National Day for Truth and Reconciliation."

continually calling us forth into new life. May our state of grace urge us to seek gracious relationships, May we see a clear path toward love.

6

THE RESPONSE TO THE WORD

THIS CHAPTER IS CONCERNED with both the theology and practice of the sacraments. I reflect on the theologies that underlie our liturgies for baptism and communion, the theologies that are implicit or explicit within our worship practices. Through preaching and liturgy we confess our theological perspectives, and we craft a particular kind of theological space for worship. There is an opportunity in both preaching and liturgy to highlight theological perspectives that help prepare us for the work of conciliation/reconciliation with Indigenous communities. I will offer both theological reflection and some liturgical resources that make space for healing and the possibility of conciliation/reconciliation. The chapter ends with a reflection on the pastoral prayer, also called the Prayers of the People, or the Prayer of Thanksgiving and Intercession.

The Sacrament of Baptism

Baptism does not take place at every worship service. The font is a visible reminder that we gather as a community of baptized persons. When the sacrament is not included in the order of worship, there should still be reminders of our baptismal identity throughout the service—in prayers, hymns, or preaching. Baptismal identity informs our entire reality as Christians. It is absolutely central to our faith and our relationship to the world around us.

Baptism assures us that we belong to God, in life and in death. Our baptismal identity is the primary identity through which we encounter the world, and it is thus the primary identity with which we approach conciliation/reconciliation with Indigenous peoples. Baptismal identity does not negate our other identities, but it is woven through our being and should ultimately determine our ethics. In other words, baptism is the basis on which we make decisions about our approach to the world around us. While baptism promotes the unity of the body of Christ, it celebrates diversity and difference within that body. Baptism connects us to others, to the whole church in all times and all places. Indigenous Christians are part of the body, and in baptism we are joined to them, just as we are joined to the whole global church. The local congregation makes promises to the child or adult being baptized, and yet those promises represent the commitment of the whole church to each child of God who enters the community through baptism. In essence, the congregation signs a blank check, promising that they will do whatever it takes to care for this new person in Christ—spiritually but also physically, materially, psychologically. Through baptism, settler Christians are intimately connected to a whole host of others who are also in the church but occupy very different positions, including Indigenous Christians. Our baptismal promises transcend the local context, and thus we share responsibility for the well-being of a whole host of baptized Christians in the larger context.

Baptism does not only prepare us for relationships within the body of Christ but also for those beyond the church. In baptism, we are caught up in God's loving embrace and sent out into the world to be ambassadors of God's reconciling love. The nature of the triune God is self-giving love that overflows the bounds of the Trinity and pours out on us. As recipients of this self-giving, we are invited to share it within the church and outside of the church. What will it mean for us to practice self-giving love in the context of settler colonialism?

When Jesus was baptized in the waters of the Jordan, God named him as God's own beloved child. This was a public declaration about Jesus' identity. What we know from Scripture is that Jesus used power in a particular way—he came alongside people rather than forcing them to comply with his beliefs. He became vulnerable, even to the point of death on the cross.

Like Jesus, we are rooted in love through baptism and prepared for interconnectedness. We too are crafted in God's image, in the image of Creator, Son, and Holy Spirit. This identity can be hard to grasp because the nature of the Trinity is so complex. The way that we interpret God's identity matters a great deal for how we approach and respond to the world around us. There has been a tendency on the part of the Western church to create God in our image instead of the other way around. God has been perceived to be male and white. This version of God has justified enslavement, colonialism, and oppression by siding with powerful groups instead of the poor and marginalized. This kind of theology provided encouragement and justification to the architects of residential schools, claiming its superiority over all other theologies and worldviews. In many cases, the goal was to use baptism as a preventative measure to rid the Indigenous child of their "heathen" practices and beliefs.

Take the example of an article written by an American, Declan Leary, in 2021, which argues that the abuses that took place at residential schools were "worth it" because they resulted in the baptisms and catechisms of many Indigenous children, thereby enlarging the mission of Christ. In his article, he claims that the discovery of children's graves is not at all scandalous and that the erasure of Indigenous culture was a good thing.

> Whatever natural good was present in the piety and community of the pagan past is an infinitesimal fraction of the grace rendered unto those pagans' descendants who have been received into the Church of Christ. Whatever sacrifices were exacted in pursuit of that grace—the suffocation of a noble pagan culture; an increase in disease and bodily death due to government negligence; even the sundering of natural families—is worth it.[1]

I wish to characterize this as an extremely noxious opinion that illustrates the dangers of any baptismal theology that creates God in our image. Baptism in Christ does not erase the identities or cultures in which it is presented. Rather, baptism preserves the diversity and difference found within the church, as it is in God's very nature to be diverse and to honor difference. Thus, we should universally condemn forced baptism especially when used as a means to destroy cultures and other identities. This article provides a good example of the ways that baptism has been misused and misunderstood by colonizers.

Baptism is a means of grace, not a prerequisite to grace, even though the Western church has often treated it as such. In baptism, we are sent out as participants in God's reconciling love—this means that our baptismal identity urges us toward relationships with others. It is because of our baptism that we are equipped and prepared to engage in conciliation/reconciliation with Indigenous peoples. As members of the body of Christ, this is something we do together—we are not alone but placed into the embrace of a loving community that transcends our own location. Rather, we partner with other Christians in other places to enact the *imago Dei* as it is present in each one of us and in the community as a whole. Despite the sinfulness that blurs the *imago Dei* within us, we are continually remade by God's grace. There is always an element of discipleship to our baptisms—we are

---

1. Leary, "Meaning of the Native Graves."

created and called for a purpose, and that purpose is to partner with God in the reconciling of the whole of creation.

Baptismal theologies place us in a particular position vis-à-vis Indigenous Christians. We have, from a distance, made promises to the children and the adults who have been baptized within Indigenous churches. Therefore, a special, albeit broken, relationship already exists among Christian settlers and Indigenous Christians. This may be a space of encounter that will allow us to listen carefully and come into relationship. While the body of Christ supports and embraces difference, faith in Jesus Christ is held in common. While this faith will be held and expressed in different ways in different communities, it gives us a shared starting point for conversation. Settler churches can offer support for Indigenous ministries that foster the well-being of the wider Indigenous community.

It is important to recognize that Christian faith may be an uncomfortable place for many Indigenous peoples, as the experience of residential schools and other societal abuses have, for some, "shattered" their Christian faith.[2] The suffering of God himself may provide a basis for the beginning of a conversation. Duane Gastant Aucoin is a Carmelite brother and a World Clan member of the Tlingit Nation in the Yukon. They write, "Just as God brought good out of the evil done to His Son after they crucified Him, by raising Him up from the dead, so too we must work with God and with each other to bring good out of the evil done to our people. So that we as a whole may be given new life and rise up from the tomb in which we have been placed, stronger and more alive than before."[3] Baptism honors this dying and rising to new life, which is a strong image for repairing the damage that has been done by the church to Indigenous peoples. In baptism, we die to our sin. Our old ways of thinking are undone and buried, while we are invited to embrace newness and possibility for renewed relationships. What aspects of our colonial mindsets need to be put to death? Rooted in baptismal identity, we are raised up as those who can imitate God's reconciling, self-giving love. Baptism may open doors for enhanced relationships in which settlers can learn much from Indigenous Christians. "In due course, Indigenous persons may choose to share their spiritual experience and to help non-Indigenous believers to deepen their understanding of the mystery of human suffering and of the gift of mercy."[4]

---

2. McDonough, "Truth and Reconciliation Commission."

3. Aucoin, "Residential Schools," 1.

4. McDonough, "Truth and Reconciliation Commission."

Baptism and Care for Creation

Indigenous peoples rightfully claim that the healing of the land is primary to the hope of conciliation/reconciliation. Baptism is an embodied practice that is enacted by water and word. Through the waters of baptism, we are tied to the whole of creation. It is within the context of our baptisms that we are called to be healers of the land.

As Margaret Bullitt-Jonas preached to one congregation, "The divine love into which we were plunged in baptism extends not only to us, and not only to human beings, but also to every sparrow and whale, every earthworm and orca, every maple tree and mountain."[5] The following words were recently added to the Anglican Church in Canada's baptismal covenant: "Will you strive to safeguard the integrity of God's creation, and respect, sustain and renew the life of the Earth?"[6] In addition to the other promises made at baptism, this promise explicitly ties our baptism to the care of creation. Indigenous theologies will identify land as one of the "relatives" to whom we are connected in every way. In baptism we are called not only to provide care for the land and its creatures but also to renew the land—to repair what has been damaged by greed and the ravages of colonialism.

Most of us turn on our kitchen taps and an abundance of safe water pours out. There is plenty of water to put in our fonts. There are dozens of Indigenous communities in Canada that live without access to clean, fresh water. The Curve Lake First Nation, for example, is surrounded by water—but the water is not potable. Chief Emily Whetung says, "The emotional and spiritual damage of not having clean water, having to look at all of the water surrounding us on a daily basis and unable to use it, is almost unquantifiable."[7] The problem is one of infrastructure, as many Indigenous communities are far-flung and it is difficult to get the water treatment facilities up and running. This problem is at least partially based in the consequences of colonial-era laws that prohibited people living on reserves from building their own access to clean water. The Canadian government, while supposedly working on the problem, has not managed to solve it and expects to take several years to do so.[8] "The auditor's review of the First Nations drinking water crisis found Indigenous Services Canada's efforts to lift boil water advisories have been constrained by a funding policy that hasn't

---

5. Bullitt-Jonas, "Baptism into the Community of Creation."
6. Hair, "Covenant and Care."
7. Cecco, "Dozens of Canada's First Nations."
8. Stefanovich et al., "Too Many First Nations."

been updated in thirty years, and by the lack of a regulatory regime that includes legal protections comparable with other communities in Canada."[9]

This current state of events is entirely rooted in racism and colonialism. Despite the importance of the creation for Indigenous people, they are excluded from access to one of Canada's greatest natural resources—water. This lack of basic human rights is only one example of the ways that colonialism continues to negatively affect Indigenous communities. In baptism, we pass through the waters on our way to new life. It is largely symbolic but also represents the fact that water is absolutely vital for sustaining life. As long as Indigenous communities are without safe and abundant water, we as a culture are failing to provide the necessities of life. We should remember this reality when we come to the font, celebrating the ways that God has used water to bring people to new life—through the waters of the Jordan, the waters of the Red Sea, the waters of baptism. As baptized people, we are invited to urge governments to repair what is broken.

Our earth is suffering, and climate change has had serious consequences for Indigenous peoples all over the world. It is not only fresh water that is a problem. It is also industrial abuse such as mining that strips the land of its natural health and deforestation that removes the trees and vegetation that literally provide the air that we breathe. The call here is to mend the land, to heal the creation. As baptized Christians, we share the task of stewarding the land, caring for it, and making it a safe place for all creation to live vibrantly and in peace. The Presbyterian Mission Organization (PCUSA) asks the question, "What can we do?" in relation to forest fires raging uncontrolled in Brazil. In response, it draws on Rom 8: "We must remember first the church's call: We are challenged by the cries of the people who suffer and by the woundedness of creation itself. We see a dramatic convergence between the suffering of the people and the damage done to the rest of creation. We have heard that creation continues to groan, in bondage, waiting for its liberation (Romans 8:22)."[10] The suffering of God's creation and the suffering of God's people are intricately related. As baptized Christians, we are called to work to heal both. In worship, we might address this through our preaching and our prayers, especially in the context of the sacrament of baptism in which we are reminded of our interconnectedness with the entire created order.

9. Stefanovich et al., "Too Many First Nations."

10. Delgado, "Addressing Climate Change."

The Lord's Supper

The sacrament of the Lord's Supper presents a particular ethical challenge. Everyone is invited, including our enemies. Victims/survivors, perpetrators, and bystanders each drink the same wine and share the same bread. We have all fallen short, and yet we have been (miraculously!) forgiven by God. As if we can't help ourselves, we sin again and again, and return to a never-ending cycle of grief, repentance, and healing. We come to the table as those who have been forgiven by God, and yet may remain in conflict with others. Matthew 5 expresses the need to be reconciled with one's neighbor before one receives the sacrament. If we are to envision Indigenous communities as neighbors, then we are certainly not reconciled as we come to the table. Within the context of a relationship, we may individually find reconciliation, but as settler communities we have not yet done the necessary work to be conciled/reconciled. So, as we come to the table we must bring with us the unanswered questions and burdens related to the oppression of Indigenous communities by the church, government, and society at large. We come, reconciled to God yet unreconciled with one another. While we are invited to come over and over, to confess and be forgiven, to feast at the table, there remains a shadow side to our joy. There are conflicts, there is terrible inequity, there is silence from those who should speak up. We bring all of those realities to the table with us, and they must be acknowledged. We come to the table as those who are unreconciled to our neighbors. This does not mean that we are unworthy but that our gift, perhaps, is incomplete.

In the sacrament, we experience firsthand the concrete provision of grace—in bread and wine we live out the act of reconciliation with God. We remember God's mighty acts and the gift of Jesus Christ and the power of the Spirit—all of which point to the lengths to which God will go to be reconciled to God's people. It is at the table that we are permitted, perhaps, to hope that reconciliation is indeed possible. From our place at Christ's table, we are granted a vision of life that dares to hope that the way things are is not the way things must be. So here, we may actually be transformed and enabled to do work that previously seemed unimaginable.

Communion in some ways provides a third space where we can encounter others. Many congregations will have an assortment of people attending their communion services—immigrants, Indigenous people, white settlers. Even if one of those groups are not present in actual fact, they are present to us because the church celebrates the sacrament with all the citizens of the kingdom of heaven. Whether or not we see them face to face, our Indigenous siblings are at that table with us. We must look them in the eye and account for the sins of past and present. The encounter, literal or figurative, is awkward and embarrassing because the truth is that the church has not done enough to protect and nurture Indigenous communities whether they are Christian or otherwise. At the table, we are forced to confront this truth, but in confronting unpleasant realties we are opening ourselves to the possibility of relationship with those we have harmed. Whether that relationship will be established is, of course, up to the Indigenous person or community.

There is a danger that our very earnest desire for reconciliation will lead to a premature proclamation of victory. We have not achieved conciliation/reconciliation with Indigenous people merely because we have sat down together at a sacred table and shared bread and wine. Rather, we have participated in a shared space in which the spirit moves, which makes room for confession, and acknowledgment, and even tears. Trusting in the power of God to move in unexpected ways, we can hope that the space of communion might become a genuine space of conversation and listening. This is not, however, reconciliation. Reconciliation involves much more than listening, much more than shared space. Indeed, reconciliation may involve turning our own lives upside down.

A tradition sometimes associated with communion is the Passing of the Peace. "The ancient position of the peace was before the presentation of bread and wine, at the beginning of the Eucharistic Prayer. The Roman tradition has changed the position to after the Eucharistic Prayer and almost immediately before taking communion."[11] Some congregations choose to include the Passing of the Peace at the very beginning of worship. It is a practice, however, that is intimately tied to the table. While I am advocating for the inclusion of the Passing of the Peace in the worship service, I will admit that I dislike the Passing of the Peace—not for any theological reason but because it makes me uncomfortable as an introvert. It is important to acknowledge that it can be uncomfortable and may not be a safe space for everyone—including those who are shy, visiting, or perceive themselves to be marginal to the community. This is a consideration for hospitality and welcome. It also raises the very real possibility that we may encounter someone in worship who does not want to share peace with us. That is their prerogative, as difficult and awkward as the moment may be. This is not to suggest in any way that we should expect hostility in the worship event, but to acknowledge that there is pain that divides and separates people, even in the midst of worship.

While the table may or may not be a space for healing relationships among settler, Indigenous, and other communities, it can still be a space

---

11. Van Ommen, "Worship, Truth, and Reconciliation," 63.

of healing for individuals and for the community. Individuals and communities express deep emotion through participation in the sacrament. God gets right in the middle of that emotion, and thus we are potentially transformed. We are invited to lay down all our burdens at the table. God is at work within us to heal those wounds that prevent us as settlers from entering into true reciprocal and respectful relationships with Indigenous communities. God can transform grief and shame, anger, anxiety, confusion, greed, and reluctance—some of the barriers that prevent us from truly seeking reconciliation.

A discussion of communion and reconciliation must include a conversation about forgiveness. Settlers may come to worship genuinely seeking the forgiveness of Indigenous peoples, and they may be disappointed if such forgiveness is not forthcoming. As stated in an earlier chapter, the assurance of pardon we receive in worship is a celebration of the forgiveness we have received from God—not from other people. God's forgiveness may inspire us and transform us to the point where we are able to forgive others who have caused us harm or to ask forgiveness from those we have caused harm. This inspiration and transformation does not always come and relationships remain broken. They remain broken because the necessary steps toward healing and reconciliation have not been taken. We should not anticipate forgiveness from an Indigenous person for the wrongs committed by the church against Indigenous populations. Nor should we anticipate forgiveness for the ways that settlers individually perpetrate or fail to protest harm against Indigenous communities by the government and private corporations. No, settlers do not have a right to forgiveness. It is rather something we may humbly hope for and earnestly work toward. I now turn to a discussion of forgiveness rooted in the work of Desmond Tutu. I believe that his work is helpful for considering the place of forgiveness in the sacrament of communion, given its emphasis on forgiveness and reconciliation following apartheid in South Africa. As has been the case throughout these chapters, I am focusing on the experience of white settlers in North America and the manner in which they can approach the topic of forgiveness in the context of communion.

Tutu reminds us that in regard to apartheid racism and its aftermath, Black and white people's histories and realities are bound up together. He believes that God has bound them, so that "one group's future is inherently dependent on the well-being of the other."[12] Our personhood is inextricably bound up in the existence of other persons. If one person's humanity is denigrated, the humanity of all is denigrated.

12. Tutu, *No Future without Forgiveness*, 8.

Restorative justice, which was characteristic of traditional African ju-
risprudence, is a unique way of viewing justice and reconciliation: "Here the
central concern is not retribution or punishment. In the spirit of ubuntu, the
central concern is the healing of breaches, the redressing of imbalances, the
restoration of broken relationships, a seeking to rehabilitate both the victim
and the perpetrator, who should be given the opportunity to be reintegrated
into the community he [sic] has injured by his offense."[13] It is not helpful,
writes Tutu, to demonize the perpetrator. "Theology said they still, despite
the awfulness of their deeds, remained children of God with the capacity
to repent, to be able to change."[14] Jesus himself spent time with the "scum
and the dregs," thus modeling the belief that change and transformation are
possible, even among the worst sinners. In this theology there is nothing,
no situation, no person, that is irredeemable. There is hope, then, that a
new reality could arise in which friendship might develop where there was
previously enmity. There is hope that the dehumanized perpetrator might
be helped to recover their lost humanity. Tutu insists, "This is not a wild
irresponsible dream. It has happened and it is happening and there is hope
that nightmares will end, hope that seemingly intractable problems will find
solutions and that God has some tremendous fellow-workers, some out-
standing partners out there."[15]

The process of forgiveness must begin with an expression of remorse,
or an apology, from the perpetrator. Theologian Miroslav Volf writes, "Genuine repentance may be one of the most difficult acts for a person, let alone
a community, to perform. For good reasons, Christian tradition thinks
of genuine repentance not as a human possibility but as a gift of God."[16]
With God's help, perpetrators are invited to lay down their burden of sin by
apologizing for the wrongs committed. This apology might not be accepted,
but it is a necessary step. It may indeed open the door for the perpetrator to
forgive themselves. In the context of Indigenous-settler relations, it is necessary for the church to express remorse and apologize for its historical and
ongoing role in oppression and injustice. It must apologize for its leadership
in residential schools, its deep participation in colonialism, and its failure to
speak out loudly about the current inequalities and suffering of Indigenous
peoples.

Another aspect of the conversation around forgiveness is the necessity of making reparation. Tutu writes, "Unless there is real material

13. Tutu, *No Future without Forgiveness*, 54–55.

14. Tutu, *No Future without Forgiveness*, 83.

15. Tutu, *No Future without Forgiveness*, 158.

16. Volf, *Exclusion and Embrace*, 119.

transformation in the lives of those who have been apartheid's victims, we might just as well kiss reconciliation goodbye. It just won't happen without some reparation."[17] The next chapter will outline some of the concrete ways that settlers might make reparation to Indigenous neighbors. It seems that there cannot be any possibility of forgiveness unless the material needs of Indigenous communities are met in such a way that suffering is reduced. At the communion table, we touch and handle things unseen, but we also celebrate the basic gifts of bread and wine. Our celebration should not ignore material needs—this is a place to ensure that all are fed and nourished not only spiritually but in concrete, physical ways. Colonialism is a practice that relates to land, resources, and physical bodies. Our celebration is incomplete if we do not ensure that all are safe and provisioned.

Tutu's book is both hopeful and realistic. He does not shy away from telling the truth, especially as it was expressed through South Africa's Truth and Reconciliation Commission. He tells brutal stories about murder, torture, and dehumanization. However, he is still able to affirm that the only way forward is through forgiveness. "There is a movement, not easily discernible, at the heart of things to reverse the awful centrifugal force of alienation, brokenness, division, hostility, and disharmony. God has set in motion a centripetal process, a moving toward the center, toward unity, harmony, goodness, peace, and justice, a process that removes barriers."[18] It is this process that we enter into at the communion table, a space of possibility in which barriers can be broken down and God can act to enable the repair of that which is broken.

As noted above, I do not believe that the time is right for settlers to ask forgiveness of Indigenous peoples, because the prerequisites for robust truth-telling, adequate reparations, and sincere apologies have not yet been met. Settlers may be able to repent and forgive themselves for their action and inaction. Laying down guilt and shame makes space within us for the even more difficult work of conciliation/reconciliation. At the communion table, our prayer is for relationship with those we have harmed. This relationship may not be desired by Indigenous peoples, and settlers must take the lead from them. Even if forgiveness and friendship are not offered to settlers by Indigenous peoples, settlers will need to continue to the work of apologizing, repairing, and hoping for a new relationship built on mutual respect.

17. Tutu, *No Future without Forgiveness*, 229.
18. Tutu, *No Future without Forgiveness*, 265.

The Prayers of the People

Whether or not the sacraments are celebrated in a particular worship service, we gather for prayer as God's people. In theory, and often in practice, we are gathered around the table and the font, drawing life from our experience of both. We pray to the God who has baptized us and fed us and to whom is offered all praise and thanksgiving. In this prayer, we pray for the world, for the church, and for ourselves, although not necessarily in that order. In many ways it is an "outward-facing" prayer—it is concerned with the needs of others, in addition to our personal needs and petitions. As a community, we give thanks for God's action in Jesus Christ, and we raise up the brokenness of the world. In the pastoral prayer, we acknowledge that God is the source of life and healing and call upon God to restore, renew, or create newness.

Here we have a tremendous opportunity to pray for Indigenous communities on a regular basis. Earlier in the worship service, we confessed our sin and our misdeeds, our participation in colonialism, and the manner in which that participation interrupts good relationships. In the Prayers of the People, we pour out our concerns and our laments to God, including the hope for conciliation/reconciliation. It is appropriate to give thanks for Indigenous neighbors, their stewardship of the land, and the ways that their cultures enrich the human experience. It is necessary to pray for the well-being of Indigenous communities. The ravages of colonialism continue to cause harm, resulting in suffering for many communities, such as the lack of access to clean water. Indigenous people are overrepresented in the prison system and face barriers to basic health care and education. There are many missing and murdered Indigenous women. These are significant concerns to be brought to God.

There are times when we will simply need to lament, as in the case of residential schools. Lives have been shattered, and it is fully appropriate to wonder "Why?" and "How long?" There is space for lament in the Prayers of the People. There is opportunity to ask God hard questions and appeal for answers. As we pray for survivors and their families and communities, we do so with the recognition that our own power to bring healing is limited. There is nothing that we can say or do that will remove the pain. We can, however, hold up that pain before God, asking that God will give us the strength to do what we can to offer friendship and nourishment to Indigenous peoples. This prayer is a space to ask God to help us nurture relationships with one another. A space to express the hope that conciliation/reconciliation is possible. While Christians are called to repair what is broken, we do so only through the grace of God.

The following is a beautiful prayer offered by the Anglican Church of Canada to honor the National Day of Truth and Reconciliation. It incorporates the language of creation and calls upon God to "show us the way" toward peace and justice in relation to the created order and Indigenous neighbors.

CELEBRANT: Creator and Redeemer, as we approach you in prayer, make us walk in beauty and balance, make us open our hearts and minds, make us speak the truth. We pray first for your Community, the Church, the Body of Christ. We pray for all our relatives in the circle of life throughout all Creation; for those chosen to be our leaders and teachers.

READER: In peace, we pray to you, Lord God,

READER: We call upon the earth, our Mother and home, with its beautiful depths, soaring heights and deep waters, its vitality and abundance of life, and together we ask that it

People: Teach us and show us the way.

READER: We call upon the mountains and tundra, the high green valleys and prairies filled with wildflowers, the snows, the summits of intense silence, and we ask that they:

People: Teach us and show us the way.

READER: We call upon the land which grows our food, the nurturing soil, the fertile fields, the abundant gardens and orchards, and we ask that they:

People: Teach us and show us the way.

READER: We call upon the forests, the great trees reaching strongly to the sky with earth in their roots and the heavens in their branches, the fir and the pine, the cedar and the maple, we ask them to:

People: Teach us and show us the way.

READER: We call upon the creatures of the fields and forests and the waters, our brothers and sisters the wolves and deer, the eagle and bear, the great whales and the fish. We ask them to:

People: Teach us and show us the way.

READER: We call upon all those who have lived on this earth, our ancestors and our friends, who dreamed the best for future generations, and upon whose lives our lives are built, and with thanksgiving, we call upon them to:

People: Teach us and show us the way.

CELEBRANT: Creator, you made the world and declared it to be good: the beauty of the trees, the softness of the air, the fragrance of the grass speaks to us; the summit of the mountains, the thunder of the sky, the rhythm of the waters speak to us; the faintness of the stars, the freshness of the morning, the

dewdrops on the flower speak to us. But above all, our heart
soars, for you speak to us in Jesus the Christ, in whose name we
offer these prayers. Amen.[19]

Another prayer, published by Kairos Canada, an ecumenical advocacy organization, expresses the position of a white settler. This prayer was prepared
for National Indigenous Peoples Day. In a reformed context, because the
prayers of the community as well as the individual are lifted up, it would be
appropriate to change the "I" to "we."

Creator God,
I come to you with a humble heart,
So grateful for Your creation,
this place I am in.
The land is full of Your glory this solstice day.
Sunlight sparkles on fresh green leaves.
Bees buzz as trees burst into bloom.
Even as dew collects on dandelion leaves,
Or raindrops gather in boiling thunderclouds,
A morning sip of lifegiving water deepens my gratitude
for the life that teams [sic] across Turtle Island.

O Creator, perfect Host,
Your care and compassion were, and are,
echoed in the generous hospitality
of the original peoples—Indigenous peoples.
But the reciprocal relationships of host and guest
have been shattered.
And the pain continues.
For the death and destruction, I pour out my sorrow in lamentations.
It is for the sins of my own heart that I seek forgiveness.
Cleanse me of the thoughts and emotions
that keep those relationships from healing—
wash away the toxic entitlement, prejudiced assumptions, defensive
disinterest.

O Creator, faithful Guide,
Show me the path towards right relations,
Shape not only my words and deeds,
but even more, my reactions and thoughts.
Open my heart to the wonder, the beauty, the gifts
of the person next to me,
the protestor on the news,
the culture so different from my own.

19. Anglican Church of Canada, "Liturgy for National Indigenous Day."

Expose my racism,
Root out my deep-seated fear of change,
That I may be healed within,
even as I try to be part of the healing of Your world.
Amen.[20]

20. Neufeldt, "Prayer of a White Settler."

7

THE SENDING

THE FINAL PORTION OF the reformed worship service is the Sending. Constance Cherry argues that the Sending tends to be overlooked in public worship, and yet it is an important aspect of the continuing conversation with God and with others. In the Sending, we are "disassembling" the worshiping community just as intentionally as we gathered them at the beginning of worship.[1] This is essentially an act of "saying goodbye"—"the way we part answers the questions of how we will be in relationship while apart, and what we will do until we meet again."[2]

The Sending demonstrates a significant moment in the worship service, where God sends us out in Christ's name and commissions us to live in a particular way based on our shared understanding of the movement of God in our midst.[3] The two main parts of the Sending are the charge and the benediction. The benediction is a blessing, a good word, that reminds us who we are and under whose care. The charge is a commission—to go out and do God's will. It reminds us that we are blessed for a purpose.

Worship does not end with the benediction. We are sent out into the world to carry on with our worship by serving the world based on our shared interpretation of the word. The worship service, as I have shown, is in many ways a rehearsal for what we do outside of the sanctuary. "Reconciliation, at the very heart of the Gospel, is rehearsed in the liturgy in many ways. The liturgy, therefore, fosters a spirituality of reconciliation. Such a spirituality

1. Cherry, *Worship Architect*, 108.
2. Cherry, *Worship Architect*, 108.
3. Cherry, *Worship Architect*, 108.

is required for engaging in the work of reconciliation."[4] This spirituality of reconciliation is formed by the liturgy itself. In our prayer, our singing, our reading of the word and interpreting it, our sacraments—all of these, if led with intention, help us to develop a spirituality that can guide us as we undertake concrete tasks to engage with Indigenous peoples and move toward conciliation/reconciliation. What posture should we take as we enter into this difficult work, and what might this work entail?

Restorative Solidarity: Healing Our Histories

Elaine Enns and Ched Myers, in their book *Healing Haunted Histories*, call for settlers to engage in the process of restorative solidarity. Solidarity is understood as "shared interests" that persist despite difference and work toward mutual liberation.[5] Enns and Myers perceive restorative solidarity as the "practice of 'response-ability' in both our 'political bodies' and the 'body politic' in which we dwell. This entails working to dismantle and heal from settler colonialism, as well as to accompany and collaborate with Indigenous communities, especially those on (or of) lands on which we've settled."[6] They offer a model for a piece of decolonization work that seeks to engage the settler in terms of "ancestral trauma, historical silences, narratives of superiority, complicity and moral injury in order to recognize and redress past (and continuing) injustices."[7] We explore our own personal and communal histories in order to dismantle colonial structures and transform our relationships.

Restorative solidarity is a posture that we as settlers may take in order to engage with Indigenous peoples in the world beyond the worship space. It is active and participatory, perhaps more so than any other aspect of worship. This will also be the most challenging offering to make as it demands the most from us. This chapter may make us uncomfortable because it asks us to make a costly offering. We are dependent on God's grace to enable us to act with integrity and generosity as we move out of the worship space and into our everyday relationships. When seen as a continuation of the liturgical experience, restorative solidarity becomes an act of worship. This chapter outlines some of the possibilities for worship leaders and congregations enacting restorative solidarity with Indigenous communities. The

---

4. Van Ommen, "Worship, Truth, and Reconciliation."

5. Enns and Myers, *Healing Haunted Histories*, 42.

6. Enns and Myers, *Healing Haunted Histories*, 43.

7. Enns and Myers, *Healing Haunted Histories*, 48.

goal is to build capacity for restorative solidarity through our worship and through our engagement with the wider world.

In order to nurture a relationship with Indigenous peoples, settlers will benefit from an examination of their own social location and positionality. In chapter 1 I explored the concept of settler colonialism and have assumed throughout this book that the readers have some sense of themselves as settlers. Some have a clear narrative about how they came into the land in which they live. Others have lost the narrative about how they came to dwell in the land they call home. As we come to this work of decolonizing and restorative solidarity, it is important that we develop a deeper understanding of what it means to be a settler in North America.

Myers and Enns employ a method of "storylines": landlines, bloodlines, and songlines. Landlines refer to the "where"—the locations in which we live, move, and have our being. These will include "our immigrant family histories, whether voluntary or forced, ancestral or personal from the country of origin to North America."[8] Land is at the heart of settler colonialism. Randy Woodley notes that there is a direct correlation between one's view of the land and how they treat women and persons of color.[9] Woodley describes the origin of North America, arguing that it "came to be by means of land theft, armed removal and relocation, forced breakup of families, the outlawing of Indigenous religion, bureaucratic policies of extermination, assimilation and racism, rape of the land."[10] An aspect of preparing for the work of conciliation/reconciliation is to come to terms with settler relationship to the land, so tracing our own histories on the land is vitally important. As Woodley notes, the church itself must come to terms with its relationship to the land: "Racism is still a part of societal life, and it shapes our perceptions, our discourses, and our relatedness. Second, peoples, including the church, live on stolen land, and initial relationships on the land were based on violence, a violence that still distorts those relationships. The church must determine a social location and understand how it affects its vision and the interest it continues to protect."[11]

Bloodlines refer to the "who," and concern our identities, including "our embodied story, what we have inherited biologically and psychically from our familial, racial, ethnic and cultural formation—including the travails or privileges, traumas and impacts, of immigrant leaving and settling, including the costs of cultural loss and assimilation into settler

---

8. Enns and Myers, *Healing Haunted Histories*, 51.

9. Woodley, *Indigenous Theology*, 65.

10. Woodley, *Indigenous Theology*, 34.

11. Woodley, *Indigenous Theology*, 71.

colonialism."[12] Settlers can review their ancestry and the ways that their families have participated in, or resisted, colonial influence. How have we been formed to be the people we are today?

Songlines form the "why" and refer to "traditions of faith and Spirit that animated resilience and redemptive practices in our ancestry and that help us work for justice and healing today."[13] How has faith been passed down within the family, and how has it shaped settler response to conciliation/reconciliation? Enns and Myers suggest that storylines break through two settler excuses to avoid doing this work. Storylines help us to avoid abstraction, when we imagine that colonialism is about systems that are too significant for us to approach or that it happened somewhere else, in another time. Storylines also help to address the excuse of exoneration—when settlers insist that they do not bear personal responsibility for a distant past from which they feel disconnected.[14] Instead, settlers are invited to make the process both personal and political—each of us has a history, and each of us must relate to others who share the land with us.

Together with practices of restorative solidarity, these "circles of story" form a holistic approach to examining settler identity in a very personal way. The goal is to remember, to "heal and defect from" the systems of colonization.[15] Some of our stories have been "disappeared" by dominant narratives, and remembering seeks to bring those lost stories to life. This is an intentional discipline that seeks to relieve sociohistorical ignorance, cultural illiteracy, emotional disassociation, and credulity (what we believe about what has happened). This is deeply personal work, and yet it is also communal because it concerns how we are in relationship with other people and the ways that our landlines, bloodlines, and songlines have crossed and overlapped in violent or redemptive ways.

Enns and Myers write with the intention of "repatriating Indigenous land and life," and name decolonizing practices as expressions of "radical love" by settlers.[16] As Christian settlers, we are invited into this work of radical love. By examining our own landlines, bloodlines, and songlines, we can begin to construct an understanding of settler identity and work toward our own decolonization and the decolonization of our churches. If we are to be equipped for the work of conciliation/reconciliation, we will benefit from a clear picture of how we came to exist on the land, the ways that trauma

12. Enns and Myers, *Healing Haunted Histories*, 51.
13. Enns and Myers, *Healing Haunted Histories*, 51.
14. Enns and Myers, *Healing Haunted Histories*, 79.
15. Enns and Myers, *Healing Haunted Histories*, 82.
16. Enns and Myers, *Healing Haunted Histories*, 325.

and blessing have inhabited our familial and community lines, and look for signs of redemption in our histories and present contexts.

Decolonizing Western Worldviews

All of us absorb the cultural realities that shape the societies in which we live, work, and worship. Western settler cultures, over time, have developed particular worldviews, perspectives that are generally shared especially within North America. There are particular priorities and values associated with these worldviews. I am intentionally using the plural in order to emphasize that even though many of these views are shared, there is a great deal of diversity in terms of how they are lived out and practiced. Generally speaking, North Americans understand themselves to be distinct from the land. They tend to value the individual over the community (including the created order). Truth is propositional, and there is a shortage of storytelling that is rooted in lived experience, because storytelling is considered to be a subjective, rather than objective, enterprise.[17] This places the head above the heart, and considers objective, provable facts to be the basis of reality rather than the heart's own experiences.[18]

Western Christianity makes a lot of promises, including civilization, development, security, and salvation, "but what is actually delivered to Indigenous peoples is imbalance, oppression, violence, and destruction."[19] The church has been engaged in projects that seek to civilize Indigenous peoples as if their own cultures have no value. It has often ignored or damaged the material and spiritual well-being of Indigenous peoples here and now while pointing to some distant future salvation that has little to do with the present. These kinds of theologies are of no earthly value, being rooted in a vision of heaven that fails to recognize the current suffering.

Indigenous theologies can assist us to deconstruct some aspects of Western worldviews. Adrian Jacobs, a Cayuga First Nation member of the Six Nations Haudenosaunee Confederacy of the Grand River Territory, proposes:

> Aboriginal culture, worldview, frame of reference, and in this case, Aboriginal Christianity, offers hope to Western missionary autism. Aboriginal people are not your problem, we are your cure. . . . We are the conscience of your technology. We are the

17. Woodley, *Indigenous Theology*, 61.
18. Woodley, *Indigenous Theology*, 67.
19. Woodley, *Indigenous Theology*, 65.

humanizers of your institutions. We matter, quite apart from your recognition of our worth. . . . We are a threat to entrenched powers-that-be who refuse to open the doors of opportunity and choice to all. We are a challenge to the mindset of greed, the avarice of Babylon, calling for the equitable distribution of resources in the spirit of the Jewish Year of Jubilee. We are good medicine for you.[20]

What can we learn from Indigenous theologies that can help us walk the path toward conciliation/reconciliation? A primary goal of missionary colonialism has been to "save" the non-Christian inhabitants of the land by inserting Western theologies into other cultures. Salvation is often concerned with the individual rather than the whole created order. We invite people into a personal relationship with Jesus but ignore the communal healing that must take place if salvation is to truly occur. In addition, as noted above, salvation tends to be about the individual's relationship to heaven, rather than focusing on salvation in the here and now. Woodley prefers the term "healing" to salvation, which should always be concerned with the healing of the land and the healing of human relationships. Woodley argues that Christ came to heal us so that we can be people who restore harmony. This restoring of harmony is a collective task. God is concerned not only with the human soul but with the whole of creation.[21]

Settlers can learn much about the healing of the land from Indigenous peoples, for whom this is a priority. It will be useful for the church to develop a robust theology of the land that takes into consideration the damage done to the land by colonial and neocolonial practices such as mining, drilling, and deforestation. We are all in relationship to the land, and that relationship has been broken by colonial practices.

Woodley describes a pattern of Indigenous perspectives that are shared among at least forty-five different tribal groups, which he calls "the harmony way."[22] This harmony way is identified by ten traits and practices that constitute the core of Indigenous spirituality. These theological perspectives offer settlers a way to think through and critique Western theological perspectives in order to propose theologies that contribute to robust relationships with Indigenous peoples.

---

20. Jacobs, "Mitigating Missionary Autism," 70.

21. Woodley, *Indigenous Theology*, 79.

22. Woodley, *Indigenous Theology*, 92. He notes that while these patterns cannot be generalized across all Indigenous groups, there is a widespread, shared pattern of practicing this "harmony way."

1. A tangible spirituality must be practiced. The land and everything that lives on it is sacred and must be respected. This points to a belief in the Great Mystery/Creator, the perspective that all creation is both natural and spiritual; continued involvement in ceremonies and traditions is important; tribal societies are vital to the flourishing of the whole community; symbols are significant and are used in everyday life; authority does not come from information or propositions but from reflection upon experience.

2. Our lives are governed by harmony. In essence, this points to a belief that human beings are mainly good, and it is in creation's best interest for human beings to seek peace, balance and harmony in everything they do.

3. Community is essential. Everyone is interrelated and sacred, including women and children. We are all members of a huge family, and we should seek to expand this circle of community.

4. Humor is sacred and necessary. In both casual and formal ways, laughing together reminds us that we are human beings. It is part of seeking balance.

5. Feeling of cooperation/communality. In this view, diversity is considered a strength, and dissension is tolerated and respected, both minds and hearts are honored, consensus gives dignity, and "everyone gets a say."

6. Oral communication and traditions. In this view, words are understood to have primordial power and should be used cautiously. Oral transmission of stories is the main way that teaching happens. Communication is quiet and respectful, and all are encouraged to "speak from the heart."

7. Present and past time orientation. There is a fluidity between the past and the present, and the future is determined by seeking wisdom from the past. In this view, what is happening in the present is more significant than what will happen in the future.

8. Open work ethic. Work should be meaningful and people should be engaged in only necessary work, leaving plenty of time for rest and the enjoyment of creation.

9. Great hospitality/generosity. Through the sharing of resources in homes, and gift-giving ceremonies, there is a hope that all will share what they have.

10. Natural connectedness to all creation. Human beings are seen as stewards of the land, or co-sustainers. As the earth sustains us, so we work to sustain the earth and its well-being. Everything is interrelated. Gratitude for the earth and all creation is expressed in ceremony.[23]

Woodley offers a caution that arises from a tendency associated with Western worldviews—to believe that all problems can be repaired, that the relationships can be "fixed." Rather than rush into the context of conciliation/reconciliation thinking we have answers, we are invited first to listen. The settler must listen to the stories of Indigenous peoples and the history of the land as it has been taught and contested.

In response to the question "What can we do?" as settlers to repair the problem, Woodley offers a brief paradigm. Once they have listened for a long time, "what White Western folks must do, both structurally and individually, is to heal the relationships between themselves, Creator, the land, and the local Indigenous peoples."[24] This begins with an awareness and a process of education in which settlers engage with Indigenous wisdom. To be clear, it is the settler's responsibility to learn, not the Indigenous person's responsibility to teach. There are plenty of resources written by Indigenous folk that will aid settlers in understanding the key issues and the barriers to conciliation/reconciliation.

Next, settlers are invited to lament together. Lament is part of what it means to become a community together. This is true in the Christian sense: Congregations are given opportunity to lament the status quo, to name before God guilt and anger, to make reparations.

Finally, Woodley writes about the importance of memorializing—of creating monuments that help us to remember our stories and the stories of others. He recalls the biblical memorials that were built when God encountered humanity in significant ways.[25] These markers enabled people to look back and remember what had happened but also to look forward. "Memorials are intended to restore relationships of the past for future generations, which means looking back to go forward. You should be asking yourselves, 'What were the original relationships supposed to be with the Creator, the land, and the Indigenous people of this area?'"[26] By remembering these original intentions of the Creator, we may come closer to being able to establish relationships with Indigenous peoples. One way of doing this is to ensure that Indigenous peoples are re-empowered to be hosts on the land

---

23. Woodley, *Indigenous Theology*, 92–94.
24. Woodley, *Indigenous Theology*, 42.
25. See Gen 31:45–46, 35:14; Josh 4:3–10.
26. Woodley, *Indigenous Theology*, 43.

with authority. We need to tear down structures that prevent Indigenous people from having agency over their own lives and land. When we do this, we are creating "monuments" that acknowledge the past but point to a better future.

Dismantling and Healing from Settler Colonialism: Seeking Shalom

I have sought to describe the ways that settler worship can be critiqued and reformed in order to move toward right relations with Indigenous peoples. As the inheritors and practitioners of settler colonialism, we will wonder what else we can do to foster stronger, more equal, and respectful relationships with Indigenous nations. Turning again to Randy Woodley, I want to present his notion of "shalom" as a positive vision for the kinds of communities that will sustain and nurture Indigenous-settler relations. Woodley relates "the harmony way" to the biblical concept of shalom, a group of words or concepts that translate as "peace, restoration of creation, prosperity, respect, justice, truth, acceptance, restitution, abundance, equity, integrity, intimacy, growth, well-being, restored relationship, and a place where God is in charge."[27]

Walter Brueggemann has this to say about shalom:

> Shalom is the end of coercion. Shalom is the end of fragmentation. Shalom is the freedom to rejoice. Shalom is the courage to live an integrated life in a community of coherence. These are not simply neat values to be added on, but they are massive protests against the central values by which our world operates. The world depends on coercion. The world depends on fragmented loyalties. The world as presently ordered depends on these very conditions, against which the gospel protects and to which it provides alternatives.[28]

This whole concept of shalom, which is related to the biblical concept of jubilee, is about caring for the most marginalized. It provides rest and freedom to those who are oppressed or enslaved. This rest and freedom are intended not only for human beings but for the whole creation.[29] Settlers have intentionally and powerfully broken shalom in terms of their relationship with Indigenous peoples. Woodley writes, "The problem of a Western

27. Woodley, *Shalom and the Community of Creation*, loc. 95.

28. Brueggemann, *Peace*, 51.

29. Woodley, *Indigenous Theology*, 96.

worldview displays itself: the way of life demonstrated by Western peoples leads to alienation from the earth, hostility toward others, and estrangement from all of creation."[30] Rather than living according to shalom, North Americans tend to be "physically dualistic, morally dualistic, essentially spiritual, religiously intolerant, individualistic, extrinsically categorical, hierarchical, competitive, greed based, utopian, White supremacist, anthropocentric, triumphalist, and patriarchal."[31] This rather damning description of Western priorities contrasts sharply with biblical and Indigenous concepts of shalom.

Woodley argues that Native American cultures often view life through a sacred circle or hoop. Without end or beginning, a circle is accessible at any point by anyone. "Our Aboriginal spiritual teachers speak of the reestablishment of the balance between human beings and the whole of creation as 'mending the hoop.' How can we come to a common truth of the history of White supremacy in order to deconstruct our own Western worldviews and to recognize the strength Indigenous people have to survive?"[32] For settlers, mending the hoop will involve embracing vulnerability rather than power. For Christian settlers, it may involve a recognition and embrace of the choice of God to become vulnerable in order to restore creation. Shalom is God's dream for humanity, a dream that resists our tendencies to divide and harm creation.[33]

What will it mean for Christian settlers in North America to practice an ethic of shalom? These are a series of suggestions gleaned from my research. This is not a complete list and possibly does not go far enough to advocate for the kind of changes that may be necessary. If settlers are to engage in true and respectful relationships with Indigenous peoples, what is required is no less than a revolution of thought and practice. It is also important to attend to Woodley's caution that the Western way is to imagine that everything can be "fixed." These actions are not undertaken in order to fix a problem but rather to bring about transformation within and beyond the Christian community that can lead to the kind of relationships that resonate with the desires of the Creator for the created order. Conciliation/reconciliation will take time, patience, persistence, and sustained intentionality.[34] All of these suggestions are valuable, and they are presented in no particular order.

1. Do our own work of decolonizing settler theologies, worship, and attitudes. This is about reshaping our personal and communal identities.

---

30. Woodley, *Indigenous Theology*, 98.

31. Woodley, *Indigenous Theology*, 98.

32. Woodley, *Indigenous Theology*, 103.

33. Woodley, *Shalom and the Community of Creation*, loc. 395.

34. Aldred, "National Day for Truth and Reconciliation."

The purpose of this book has been to evaluate worship and offer suggestions about how decolonizing patterns can be integrated into our own congregational life. Ray Aldred has spoken about the need for settler churches to develop emotional intelligence, and this may be a key point especially for reformed churches. The reformed tradition has a tendency to focus on the head rather than the heart. Aldred argues that emotions lead to healing. Churches that neglect the heart fail to make room for emotion and thus miss an opportunity for healing. Churches must make space for those who are "half-healed."[35] "Churches should embrace emotion and use that emotional energy to connect so we can move toward harmony with the land, with each other, with the Creator."[36]

Aldred also says that the hardest thing to reconcile is yourself.[37] This is both personal and collective work that must address our relationships to the land, to the Creator, to each other, and to ourselves. Genesis 3 presents four types of relationship—with God, Creation, others, and the self.[38] All of these kinds of relationship are essential, and I suspect that this work of reconciling these relationships must be done simultaneously, although by no means all at once. God has already reconciled Godself to us, and through God's action in Jesus Christ we have been given resources to heal every other relationship.

2. Heal the land and our relationship to the earth and the whole created order. As Ray Aldred notes, there is a wound on the land specifically caused by residential schools, which have left the bones of thousands of children to lie within the earth. These graves cry out prophetically to us to heal the land and ourselves.[39] There is much to be said about creation wounds and the way the land has been harmed through the ravages of colonialism, but there is not enough space here to do the topic justice. Let us be tied to the land on which we live, recognize our dependence upon the land, and fight to reverse the harm that has been done both to the land and people living in the land.

3. Build relationships with Indigenous peoples. Trust can be cultivated when settlers show up, listen, and show a willingness to honor the needs of Indigenous neighbors. This is not about "feeling sorry" for Indigenous peoples; it is about honoring everything they bring to the table as equal conversation partners who are empowered to tell their stories, be heard, and be given a thoughtful response. Communication is central to this endeavor

35. Aldred, "Master Class," Sep 22, 2021.
36. Aldred, "Master Class," Sep 22, 2021.
37. Aldred, "Master Class," Oct 20, 2021.
38. Aldred, "Master Class," Oct 20, 2021.
39. Aldred, "Master Class," Sep 22, 2021.

of creating intimacy and solidarity. For settlers in North America, building these kinds of relationship may be among the most difficult actions to pursue because we live such fragmented lives and are so alienated from community that many of us will have no relationships of significance with Indigenous communities.

How might we go about building such relationships if we do not know any Indigenous persons? We can prepare ourselves to be ready to engage in such relationships simply by paying attention to the Indigenous voices around us. Through social and print media we can listen to and learn from Indigenous thought leaders—we can read books by Indigenous authors, listen to podcasts, watch movies created within Indigenous communities. While this may be a "lazy" way to engage, it is at least a start. Within the Christian community, we have opportunities to relate to Indigenous Christians within our denominations. As followers of Jesus Christ, we at least have a starting point for building genuine relationships. Christian unity is a difficult subject when considered in light of colonialism because colonialism has forced a particular kind of unity that ignores difference and diversity. Instead, we are invited to honor diversity, especially within the church, and this involves honoring the distinctive Indigenous voices calling for shalom. As in any relationship, it is important that Indigenous boundaries are respected and that we do not cross these boundaries without permission.

4. Become educated. To decolonize Christian practice means to develop a deeper understanding of other worldviews and cultures. Woodley describes an experience in which settler lives are changed by a significant interaction with Indigenous practices.

> I've been running a sweat lodge for over thirty years and have hosted some hardcore White folks, people who we would consider "double-White" folks, European descended folks who exhibit all the characteristics of the privilege of Whiteness. They have come to visit our sweat lodge, and their whole lives have been changed in one night. I think it's because they've not had the opportunity to experience a whole expression of their faith or their spirituality up until that point. The structures that they've been living in, as followers of Jesus, as Christians, have not provided that experience of wholeness for them. It behooves educational institutions, and anybody associated with the church really, to provide those kinds of experiences.[40]

Settlers will need to step out of their comfort zones and form relationships with Indigenous communities so that they may be invited to participate in

40. Woodley, *Indigenous Theology*, 123.

these experiences. When we are open to experiencing the culture of another, we are more likely to be able to enter into relationship.

5. Advocate for the agency of Indigenous peoples. One of the consequences of colonialism has been to remove the agency and create dependence.[41] Settlers can get active by protesting, demonstrating, writing letters,
and supporting organizations whose purpose is to uplift the processes of
conciliation/reconciliation. Much of what is needed is political in nature—
critiquing systems and governments that get in the way of conciliation/rec-
onciliation, including unjust ecclesial structures. It is necessary for settlers
to advocate for Indigenous justice.

41. Woodley, *Indigenous Theology*, 120.

CONCLUSION

The Gathering

AT THE END, WE come back to the beginning. Worship is not a discrete event; it is a cycle and a rhythm that shapes our lives of faith. After we have been sent out into the world we are called back again into a pattern of doxology, to bring our lives to God and be reshaped and sent out again. Each time we gather for worship we have an opportunity to report on what we have seen God doing in the world, to interpret that action together, and to consider how to align ourselves with God's movement.

This book has argued that worship prepares us for the work of conciliation/reconciliation with Indigenous communities. The degree to which worship equips us will depend on the care that is taken in planning and leading worship. I have presented a series of ideas about how that might play out in live worship. It is my hope that these ideas will provide some inspiration for those who wish to reform their worship spaces and patterns so that they are more welcoming and inclusive to Indigenous peoples. Alterations to our patterns of worship are a very small step toward conciliation/reconciliation, but the hope is that these alterations will change the way that settlers perceive the tasks related to building right relations. Settlers may be able to see themselves as creatures of God who have been lovingly pulled into a reconciling love that is powerful enough to bring lasting change. Rooted in our baptismal creation story, Christian settlers may be able to enter the process of conciliation/reconciliation with the knowledge that we are called into the process by the God who is making all things new, including the relationships among Indigenous peoples and settlers.

There are many questions that have emerged in the writing of this volume. It is my hope that this book will prompt an ongoing conversation about settler-dominant congregations and their responsibility to act. While I have relied on the fourfold order of reformed worship, I have not addressed the ways that reformed worship theology may itself be steeped in colonialism. Do the very structures of worship need to be reformed in order to create spaces of welcome and hospitality?

Another question is whether the church can create sufficiently safe spaces in which Indigenous peoples will be fully welcomed and included. In chapter 2 I outlined some of the barriers that exist within the worship space. What are those barriers that prevent mutual hospitality among Indigenous peoples and settlers? How will we deal with fragility in the congregation? Is safe space even possible? I would argue that if conciliation/reconciliation are to occur, churches must be sufficiently safe in order to nurture relationship. It will require a great deal of thought and care to heal our worship spaces.

The visit of Pope Francis to Canada in summer 2022 led to a variety of responses from both Indigenous persons and settlers. The Pope chose not to rescind the Doctrine of Discovery, instead offering a somewhat lukewarm apology for the church's role in residential schools. The Pope's visit and apology was also an invitation to affirm and practice Catholic norms and values. The pattern is offense-harm-forgiveness-absolution. The assumption that forgiveness can follow harm is a large assumption, and one wonders how absolution can occur without adequate confession and truth-telling. Indigenous peoples, including Indigenous Christians, are not bound to follow the church's doctrine about forgiveness and absolution. There are other paths toward conciliation/reconciliation than the one offered by the church. Settlers have much to learn about pathways that can lead to right relationship.

I have attempted to show that settlers have agency when it comes to healing broken relationships. I have struggled, however, with the notion that settlers are "ambassadors of reconciliation." To position them as such seems to imply that settlers are uniquely qualified to do the work of conciliation/reconciliation. This positioning also implies that settlers can be the "bestower" of grace, which has strong colonial overtones. The church has failed spectacularly in its role as an ambassador of reconciliation, relying instead on violence and forced assimilation. It may be useful to remind ourselves that our participation in God's reconciling work is flawed. Indigenous Christians have shouldered the burden of conciliation/reconciliation, and settlers have much to learn from their approach. The church must be careful not to assume that it has special knowledge about how to heal these relationships. While we have experienced God's forgiving and reconciling love and are called to share it with others, we do so in limited ways. We are ambassadors, but subject to the continual illumination of the Holy Spirit and correction by our Indigenous siblings. The role of ambassador is not a high and mighty position; instead it calls us to humility, compassion, and an awareness that settlers do not have all the answers. We have received sufficient grace to participate in a conversation in which we can share what we understand about God's love. Settler understandings are not complete or authoritative but thoughtful guesses about the nature of God and God's action in the world through Jesus Christ. These "guesses" are tested and proven only in conversation with others. Perhaps it is helpful to look at the actual responsibilities of an ambassador in public service—their role is to maintain diplomatic relationships. As ambassadors, settlers are tasked with opening lines of communication, so that the love of God may be exhibited through open dialogue and mutual respect.

I have presented a fine balance here between the agency of human beings to improve the social situation and the truth that we cannot do any of this by ourselves. The divine Spirit of the Creator moves among us, repairing that which is broken and lifting our eyes toward hope. Worship begins and ends with the knowledge that God is the source and goal of worship. It is only by grace that we enter a space of worship. It is only by grace that we are transformed by that encounter with God. It is only by grace that we can imagine a future in which both settlers and Indigenous peoples can live well on the land. While God is acting graciously to bring about reconciliation, we are invited to join the work. We do this by Christ's example and at his command—"Love one another."

Isaiah paints a picture of a gathering on God's holy mountain—a vision of exiles returned, where those in power yield that power for the greater good, and creatures who do not normally find friendship are portrayed as snuggling together without animosity.

> The wolf shall live with the lamb,
>   the leopard shall lie down with the kid,
> the calf and the lion and the fatling together,
>   and a little child shall lead them.
> The cow and the bear shall graze,
>   their young shall lie down together.
>   and the lion shall eat straw like the ox.
> The nursing child shall play over the hole of the asp,
>   and the weaned child shall put its hand on the adder's den.
> They will not hurt or destroy
>   on all my holy mountain;
> for the earth will be full of the knowledge of the Lord
>   as the waters cover the sea.[1]

---

1. Isa 11:6–9.

In Isaiah's vision, the earth understands God so intimately that it will be able to live in harmony. Children, the least powerful individuals, will be safe and protected. Beasts will honor one another without tearing each other apart. Isaiah's vision is eschatological in that we cannot imagine it taking place in our lifetimes. I want to share another image of worship in which God's people gather together on God's holy mountain. I am not sure this vision is attainable or possible, but it is a vision born of hope that God can transform even the most contentious relationships. It's not a vision for an eschatological future, but a vision of what life could be like for us in the church if we embrace the work of conciliation/reconciliation.

Imagine a gathering of folks, Indigenous and settler. Coming from all directions of the earth, bringing with them their own languages and customs. Each language and custom is welcome, and each person takes their place at a long table groaning with food—bannocks and baguettes—with jugs of fresh, clear water and sweet wine. This table belongs only to Jesus Christ; it is not on land owned by anyone but everyone recognizes the history of the land and how it has been cultivated and enjoyed first by Indigenous peoples and later shared by settlers. At this table, there is conversation. We talk about the painful things and the joyful things. We talk about our relationship and its failures. We confess the ways we have caused harm. We listen to each other carefully, being truthful about our emotions and our reactions. All are heard and included in the conversation. It is a place of honesty where we delve into the Scriptures together and honor multiple interpretations. We sing in many languages, taking the time to teach each other the subtleties of pronunciation. Each person brings an offering of food or time or talent, and each gift is valued. This gathering is animated not by the suppression of difference but by its celebration. While power differences persist, there is an awareness that power needs to be configured differently within this community. There is room for negotiation.

This will not be an easy or comfortable space, but it will be a space of grace and transformation. It will not necessarily feel like a safe space for everybody because of the history of pain and violence. It is, however, a beginning. A place to cultivate relationships, where we are not limited by the voices which claim that change is not possible. The great mystery of God's grace is that it changes us even when change does not seem possible. It heals us even when healing does not seem possible. We are called to worship—to bring the best and the worst of who we are so that we may be transformed. In that space, the potential arises for relationships that can be sustained in spite of, or perhaps because of, truth-telling, confession, and restitution. Worship is the space of the triune God who is continually making us new.

There is no magic solution to the problem of settlers and their continued presence on the land. It will take immense imagination and creativity if we are to be released from destructive patterns of relationship with Indigenous populations. Thankfully, in worship we are offered immense imagination and creativity. We are made ready to love. Thanks be to God.

Charge and Benediction

In the name of the Creator, the Son, and the Spirit, go into the world:

> To love. To be loved. To never forget your own insignificance. To never get used to the unspeakable violence and the vulgar disparity of life around you. To seek joy in the saddest places. To pursue beauty to its lair. To never simplify what is complicated or complicate what is simple. To respect strength, never power. Above all, to watch. To try and understand. To never look away. And never, never to forget.[2]

---

2. Roy, *Cost of Living.*

BIBLIOGRAPHY

Alary, Laura. "Shannen and the Attawapiskat School." In "A Time for Hope: Worship Resources on the TRC Calls to Action and the United Nations Declaration on the Rights of Indigenous Peoples." The Presbyterian Church in Canada. May 2016. https://presbyterian.ca/wp-content/uploads/A-Time-for-Hope.pdf.

Aldred, Ray. "Canadian Indigenous Realities and the Canadian Church." Online lectures. Fall 2021. Food for the Hungry Canada.

———. "National Day for Truth and Reconciliation." Online lecture. September 15, 2021.

Andraos, Michel, ed. *The Church and Indigenous Peoples in the Americas: In between Reconciliation and Decolonization.* Studies in World Catholicism 7. Eugene, OR: Cascade, 2019.

Anglican Church of Canada. "A Liturgy for the National Indigenous Day of Prayer." https://www.anglican.ca/wp-content/uploads/nidp-liturgy.pdf.

———. "National Indigenous Day of Prayer." https://www.anglican.ca/im/nidp/.

âpihtawikosisân. "Settling on a Name: Names for Non-Indigenous Canadians." https://apihtawikosisan.com/2020/02/settling-on-a-name-names-for-non-indigenous-canadians/.

Aucoin, Duane Gastant. "Residential Schools." In *The Church and Indigenous Peoples in the Americas: In between Reconciliation and Decolonization*, edited by Michel Andraos, 56–77. Studies in World Catholicism 7. Eugene, OR: Cascade, 2019.

Baldwin, Jennifer. *Trauma-Sensitive Theology: Thinking Theologically in the Era of Trauma.* Eugene, OR: Cascade, 2018.

Bejan, Raluca. "Robin DiAngelo's 'White Fragility' Ignores the Differences within Whiteness." *The Conversation*, August 27, 2020. https://theconversation.com/robin-diangelos-white-fragility-ignores-the-differences-within-whiteness-143728. Accessed February 11, 2021.

Bell, John. "'Sing a New Song': Interview with Christian Century." *Christian Century* 123:15 (2006) 20–23.

Berge, Kåre. "The Empire, the Local, and Its Mediators: Deuteronomy." In *Postcolonial Commentary and the Old Testament*, edited by H. Gossai, 88–105. London: T. & T. Clark, 2018.

Berryman, Jerome. *The Complete Guide to Godly Play.* Denver: Morehouse Education Resources, 2006.

Brett, Mark G. *Decolonizing God: The Bible in the Tides of Empire.* Sheffield: Sheffield Phoenix, 2008.

Brown, Sally A., and Luke Powery. *Ways of the Word: Learning to Preach for Your Time and Place*. Minneapolis: Fortress, 2016. Kindle ed.

Brueggemann, Walter. *Peace: Living toward a Vision*. St. Louis: Chalice, 2001.

Bullitt-Jonas, Margaret. "Baptism into the Community of Creation." *Reviving Creation*. https://revivingcreation.org/baptism-into-the-community-of-creation/.

Calvin Institute of Christian Worship. "Ten Core Convictions." https://worship.calvin.edu/resources/resource-library/ten-core-convictions/.

Carvalhaes, Cláudio. *Liturgies from Below: Praying with People at the Ends of the World*. Abingdon, 2020. Kindle ed.

———, ed. *Liturgy in Postcolonial Perspectives: Only One Is Holy*. 1st ed. New York: Palgrave Macmillan, 2015.

Cecco, Leyland. "Dozens of Canada's First Nations Lack Drinking Water: 'Unacceptable in a Country So Rich.'" *Guardian*, April 30, 2021. https://www.theguardian.com/world/2021/apr/30/canada-first-nations-justin-trudeau-drinking-water.

Charles, Mark, and Soong-Chan Rah. *Unsettling Truths: The Ongoing, Dehumanizing Legacy of the Doctrine of Discovery*. Downers Grove, IL: InterVarsity, 2019. Kindle ed.

Cherry, Constance M. *The Worship Architect: A Blueprint for Designing Culturally Relevant and Biblically Faithful Services*. Grand Rapids: Baker Academic, 2010.

Cornell, Stephen, and Joseph P. Kalt. "Two Approaches to the Development of Native Nations: One Works the Other Doesn't." In *Rebuilding Native Nations: Strategies for Governance and Development*, edited by Miriam Jorgensen, 6. Tucson: University of Arizona Press, 2007.

Delgado, Yenny. "Addressing Climate Change Requires Reconciliation with Indigenous Communities." *Presbyterian Mission*, February 11, 2020. https://www.presbyterianmission.org/story/addressing-climate-change-requires-reconciliation-with-indigenous-communities/.

DiAngelo, Robin J. *White Fragility: Why It's So Hard for White People to Talk about Racism*. Boston: Beacon, 2018.

Donaldson, Laura E. "Joshua in America: On Cowboys, Canaanites and Indians." In *The Calling of the Nations: Exegesis, Ethnography, and Empire in a Biblical-Historic Present*, edited by Mark Vessey, 273–90. Toronto: University of Toronto Press, 2011.

Eiesland, Nancy. *The Disabled God: Toward a Liberatory Theology of Disability*. Nashville: Abingdon, 1994.

Energeticcity Staff. "Gentle Truth-Telling: How to Talk to Our Youngest Community Members about Residential Schools." *Energeticcity*, July 9, 2021. https://energeticcity.ca/2021/07/09/gentle-truth-telling-how-to-talk-to-our-youngest-community-members-about-residential-schools/.

Enns, Elaine, and Ched Myers. *Healing Haunted Histories: A Settler Discipleship of Decolonization*. Center and Library for the Bible and Social Justice 2. Eugene, OR: Cascade, 2021.

Epp, Roger. "We Are all Treaty People: History, Reconciliation and the 'Settler Problem.'" In *Dilemmas of Reconciliation: Cases and Concepts*, edited by Carol A. L. Prager and Trudy Govier. 223–244. Waterloo: Wilfred Laurier University Press, 2003. Kindle ed.

Gaines-Cirelli, Ginger. *Sacred Resistance: A Practical Guide to Christian Witness and Dissent*. Nashville: Abingdon, 2018. Kindle ed.

Gilio-Whitaker, Dina. "Settler Fragility: Why Settler Privilege Is So Difficult to Talk About." *Beacon Broadside* (blog), November 14, 2018. https://www. beaconbroadside.com/broadside/2018/11/settler-fragility-why-settler-privilege-is-so-hard-to-talk-about.html.

González, Catherine, and Justo González. "The Larger Context." In *Preaching as a Social Act: Theory and Practice*, edited by Art Van Seters, 29–54. Nashville: Abingdon, 1988.

Government of Canada. Indian Residential Schools Settlement Agreement. https://www.rcaanc-cirnac.gc.ca/eng/1100100015576/1571581687074.

Hair, Jesse. "Covenant and Care—A Baptismal Promise to Safeguard Creation." Anglican Church of Canada. September 6, 2013. https://www.anglican.ca/news/covenant-and-care-a-baptismal-promise-to-safeguard-creation/3006799/.

Hall, Douglas John. *The Confessing Church*. Minneapolis: Fortress, 1996.

Havea, Jione, and Collin Cowan. *Scripture and Resistance*. Edited by Jione Havea. Lanham, MD: Lexington, 2019.

Heschel, Abraham Joshua. "On Prayer." In *Moral Grandeur and Spiritual Audacity*, edited by Susannah Heschel, 257–67. New York: Farrar, Straus and Giroux, 1996.

Jacobs, Adrian. "Mitigating Missionary Autism: A Proposal for an Aboriginal Cure." *Journal of NAIITS* 9 (2011) 63, 70.

Jagessar, Michael N., and Stephen Burns. *Christian Worship: Postcolonial Perspectives*. London: Routledge, 2014. Kindle ed.

Jennings, Willie James. *The Christian Imagination: Theology and the Origins of Race*. New Haven, CT: Yale University Press, 2010. Kindle ed.

Jones, Rick. "Decolonizing Congregational Life." Presbyterian Church (USA). December 10, 2020. https://www.pcusa.org/news/2020/12/10/decolonizing-congregational-life/.

Jones, Serene. *Trauma and Grace: Theology in a Ruptured World*. Louisville, KY: Westminster John Knox, 2009.

Kairos Canada. "An Ecumenical Statement on the United Nations Declaration on the Rights of Indigenous Peoples: Responding to the Truth and Reconciliation Commission's Call to Action 48." https://www.kairoscanada.org/wp-content/uploads/2016/03/Ecumenical-Statement-EN.pdf.

———. "On the Path to Reconciliation: Kairos Worship Resources to Mark the Official Close of the Truth and Reconciliation Commission." https://www.kairoscanada.org/wp-content/uploads/2015/04/TRC-worship-May31.pdf.

Kaur, Harmeet. "Land Acknowledgements Are Often an Empty Gesture, Some Indigenous People Say." CNN, November 22, 2021. https://www.cnn.com/2021/11/22/us/native-americans-land-acknowledgments-cec/index.html.

Kim, Matthew D. *Preaching to People in Pain: How Suffering Can Shape Your Sermons and Connect with Your Congregation*. Grand Rapids: Baker Academic, 2021. Kindle ed.

Knox College. "Vision and Values." https://knox.utoronto.ca/vision-values/.

Leary, Declan. "The Meaning of the Native Graves." *American Conservative*, July 8, 2021. https://www.theamericanconservative.com/articles/the-meaning-of-the-native-graves/.

Lowman, Emma Battell, and Adam J. Barker. *Settler: Identity and Colonialism in 21st Century Canada*. Halifax: Fernwood, 2015.

Macdonald, John A. *Official Report of the Debates of the House of Commons of the Dominion of Canada*. May 9, 1883, 1107–8. Ottawa: MacLean, Roger, 1883. https://www.canadiana.ca/view/oocihm.9_07186_1_2/369.

Manuel, Arthur, et al. *Unsettling Canada: A National Wake-Up Call*. 2nd ed. Toronto: Between the Lines, 2021.

McDonough, Brian. "The Truth and Reconciliation Commission of Canada." In *The Church and Indigenous Peoples in the Americas: In between Reconciliation and Decolonization*, edited by Michel Andraos, 56–77. Studies in World Catholicism 7. Eugene, OR: Cascade, 2019.

Mitchell, Christine. "What to Do with All These Canaanites: A Settler-Canadian Reading of Biblical Conquest Stories." In *Honouring the Declaration: Church Commitments to Reconciliation and the United Nations Declaration on the Rights of Indigenous Peoples*, edited by Don Schweitzer and Paul L. Gareau, 73–98. Regina, SK: University of Regina Press, 2021.

Mitchell, Terry. "Colonial Trauma: Complex, Continuous, Collective, Cumulative and Compounding Effects on the Health of Indigenous Peoples in Canada and Beyond." *International Journal of Indigenous Health* 14:2 (2019) 74–94.

Myers, Ched, and Elaine Enns. *Ambassadors of Reconciliation*. Maryknoll, NY: Orbis, 2009.

Neufeldt, Shannon. "Prayer of a White Settler on National Indigenous Peoples Day 2020." Kairos Canada. June 15, 2020. https://www.kairoscanada.org/prayer-of-a-white-settler-on-national-indigenous-day-2020.

Presbyterian Church in Canada. "The Confession of the Presbyterian Church in Canada." https://presbyterian.ca/healing/.

———. *Living Faith: A Statement of Christian Belief*. https://presbyterian.ca/resources/resources-od/.

———. "Reconciliation Activities for Children." https://presbyterian.ca/wp-content/uploads/Reconciliation_Activities_for_Children_revised.pdf.

———. "A Time for Hope: Worship Resources on the TRC Calls to Action and the United Nations Declaration on the Rights of Indigenous Peoples." https://presbyterian.ca/wp-content/uploads/A-Time-for-Hope.pdf.

Presbyterian Church (U.S.A.). "Sense of Place." https://www.presbyterianmission.org/wp-content/uploads/sites/9/earthday2018_pc.pdf.

Procter-Smith, Marjorie. "Reorganizing Victimization: The Intersection between Liturgy and Domestic Violence." *Perkins Journal* 40:4 (1987) 17–27.

Regan, Paulette. *Unsettling the Settler within Indian Residential Schools, Truth Telling, and Reconciliation in Canada*. Vancouver: University of British Columbia Press, 2010.

Rice, Howard L., and James C. Huffstutler. *Reformed Worship*. 1st ed. Louisville, KY: Geneva, 2001.

Roy, Arundhati. *The Cost of Living*. New York: Modern Library, 1999.

Sancken, Joni S. *Words That Heal: Preaching Hope to Wounded Souls*. Nashville: Abingdon, 2019. Kindle ed.

Schiedel, Bonnie. "Why Our Kids Need to Learn about Residential Schools." *Today's Parent*. Originally published May 15, 2020. Updated May 25, 2023. https://www.todaysparent.com/kids/school-age/why-our-kids-need-to-learn-about-residential-schools/.

Schweitzer, Don, and Paul L. Gareau, eds. *Honouring the Declaration: Church Commitments to Reconciliation and the United Nations Declaration on the Rights of Indigenous Peoples*. Regina, SK: University of Regina Press, 2021.

Stefanovich, Olivia, et al. "Too Many First Nations Lack Clean Drinking Water and It's Ottawa's Fault, Says Auditor General." CBC, February 25, 2011. https://www.cbc.ca/news/politics/auditor-general-reports-2021–1.5927572.

Sugirtharajah, R. S. "The First, Second and Third Letters of John." In *A Postcolonial Commentary on the New Testament Writings*, edited by R. S. Sugirtharajah, 413–23. London: T. & T. Clark, 2007.

Titley, Brian. *A Narrow Vision: Duncan Campbell Scott and the Administration of Indian Affairs in Canada*. Toronto: University of Toronto Press, 1986.

Travis, Sarah. *Decolonizing Preaching: Decolonizing Preaching the Pulpit as Postcolonial Space*. Lloyd John Ogilvie Institute of Preaching 6. Eugene, OR: Cascade, 2014.

———. "Sermon." Knox College, National Day for Truth and Reconciliation, September 30, 2021.

Travis, Sarah, and Paul Scott Wilson. *Unspeakable: Preaching and Trauma-Informed Theology*. Eugene, OR: Cascade, 2021.

Truth and Reconciliation Commission of Canada. "Calls to Action." 2015. https://www2.gov.bc.ca/assets/gov/british-columbians-our-governments/indigenous-people/aboriginal-peoples-documents/calls_to_action_english2.pdf.

———. *Canada's Residential Schools: The Final Report of the Truth and Reconciliation Commission of Canada*. Montreal: McGill-Queen's University Press, 2016.

Tuck, Eve, and K. Wayne Yang. "Decolonization Is Not a Metaphor." *Indigeneity, Education and Society* 1:1 (2021) 1–40.

Tutu, Desmond. *No Future without Forgiveness*. New York: Crown, 1999.

Tutu, Desmond, et al. *The Book of Forgiving: The Fourfold Path for Healing Ourselves and Our World*. Edited by Douglas Carlton Abrams. 1st ed. New York: HarperOne, 2014.

United Nations General Assembly. United Nations Declaration on the Rights of Indigenous Peoples (UNDRIP). Resolution 61/295. September 13, 2007. https://www.un.org/development/desa/indigenouspeoples/wp-content/uploads/sites/19/2018/11/UNDRIP_E_web.pdf.

United Nations Permanent Forum on Indigenous Peoples. "Who Are Indigenous Peoples?" Indigenous People, Indigenous Voices: Factsheet. https://www.un.org/esa/socdev/unpfii/documents/5session_factsheet1.pdf.

Van der Kolk, Bessel A. *The Body Keeps the Score: Brain, Mind, and Body in the Healing of Trauma*. New York: Viking, 2014.

Van Ommen, Armand Léon. "Worship, Truth, and Reconciliation: A Liturgical Spirituality of Peace-Making." *Liturgy* 34:1 (2019) 58–66.

Vessey, Mark, ed. *The Calling of the Nations: Exegesis, Ethnography, and Empire in a Biblical-Historic Present*. Toronto: University of Toronto Press, 2011.

Volf, Miroslav. *Exclusion and Embrace: A Theological Exploration of Identity, Otherness, and Reconciliation*. Nashville: Abingdon, 2019.

Waldman, Katy. "A Sociologist Examines the 'White Fragility' That Prevents White Americans from Confronting Racism." *New Yorker*, July 23, 2018. https://www.newyorker.com/books/page-turner/a-sociologist-examines-the-white-fragility-that-prevents-white-americans-from-confronting-racism. Accessed Feb 5, 2021.

Wallis, Maria A., et al. *Colonialism and Racism in Canada: Historical Traces and Contemporary Issues*. Toronto: Nelson Education, 2010.

Warrior, Robert Allan. "Canaanites, Cowboys and Indians: Deliverance, Conquest and Liberation Theology Today." *Christianity and Crisis* 49:12 (1989) 261–65.

White, Victoria Atkinson. "The Hope of Traditioned Innovation." PhD diss., Duke University, 2016. https://hdl.handle.net/10161/13617.

Whitla, Becca. *Liberation, (De)Coloniality, and Liturgical Practices: Flipping the Song Bird*. 1st ed. Cham, Switzerland: Palgrave Macmillan, 2020.

Winner, Lauren F. *The Dangers of Christian Practice: On Wayward Gifts, Characteristic Damage, and Sin*. New Haven, CT: Yale University Press, 2018.

Woodley, Randy S. *Indigenous Theology and the Western Worldview*. Acadia Studies in Bible and Theology. Grand Rapids: Baker Academic, 2022.

———. *Shalom and the Community of Creation: An Indigenous Vision*. Grand Rapids: Eerdmans, 2012. Kindle ed.

World Council of Churches. "Statement on the Doctrine of Discovery and Its Enduring Impact on Indigenous Peoples." February 17, 2012. https://www.oikoumene. org/resources/documents/statement-on-the-doctrine-of-discovery-and-its-enduring-impact-on-indigenous-peoples.

Wymer, Andrew. "Introduction: Liturgy as Protest and Resistance." *Liturgy* 35:1 (2020) 1–2. https://doi.org/10.1080/0458063X.2020.1701886.

———. "The Liturgical Intersection of Harm and Healing: The Problems of Necessary and Unnecessary Liturgical Violence and Their Unmaking through Liturgical Healing." https://religiouseducation.net/rea2014/files/2014/07/RIG-Wymer.pdf.

Yerxa, Jana-Rae. "Refuse to Live Quietly!" Indigenous Nationhood Movement, 2014. http://nationrising.org/refuse-to-live-quietly/.

York, Geoffrey, and Loreen Pindera. *People of the Pines: the Warriors and the Legacy of Oka*. Toronto: McArthur, 1999.